Marc Serota

About the Author

NORMAN F. CANTOR was Emeritus Professor of History,
Sociology, and Comparative Literature at New York
University. His academic honors included appointments
as a Rhodes Scholar, Porter Ogden Jacobus Fellow at
Princeton University, and Fulbright Professor at Tel Aviv
University. His many books include the *New York Times*
bestseller *In the Wake of the Plague, Antiquity, Inventing
the Middle Ages* (nominated for a National Book Critics
Circle Award), and *The Civilization of the Middle Ages*,
the most widely read narrative of the Middle Ages in the
English language.

^{the} Last Knight

· NORMAN F. CANTOR ·

the Last Knight

THE TWILIGHT OF THE MIDDLE AGES AND THE BIRTH OF THE MODERN ERA

PICTURE EDITOR: JUDY CANTOR

HARPER
PERENNIAL

HARPER ● PERENNIAL

A hardcover edition of this book was published in 2004 by the Free Press.

HarperCollins books may be purchased for educational, business, or sales promo-
tional use. For information please write: Special Markets Department, Harper-
Collins Publishers, 10 East 53rd Street, New York, NY 10022.

FIRST HARPER PERENNIAL EDITION PUBLISHED 2005.

Library of Congress Cataloging-in-Publication Data
Cantor, Norman F.
  The last knight : the twilight of the Middle Ages and the birth of the modern
  era / by Norman F. Cantor ; picture editor, Judy Cantor.— 1st Harper Perennial ed.
    p. cm.
  Originally published: New York : Free Press, c2004.
  Includes bibliographical references and index.
  ISBN 0-06-075403-6
  ISBN-13: 978-0-06-075403-7
  1. Middle Ages—History. 2. Europe—History—476–1492. 3. Civilization,
  Medieval—14th century. 4. John, of Gaunt, Duke of Lancaster, 1340–1399.
  5. Nobility—Great Britain—Biography. I. Title.

D202.8.C36 2005
942.03'7'092—dc22
[B]   2005040607

05 06 07 08 09 ❖/RRD 10 9 8 7 6 5 4 3 2 1

To my family

Acknowledgments

I wish to thank Ms. Dee Ranieri for typing the manuscript and preparing the disk for the publisher.

My literary agent, Alexander Hoyt, and my editor at Free Press, Bruce Nichols, have been very helpful in shaping the manuscript.

Contents

Plantagenet Family Dynasty

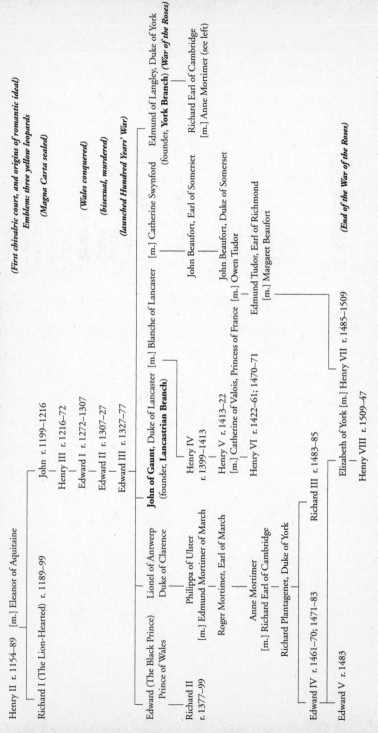

the Last Knight

Introduction

JOHN OF GAUNT, Duke of Lancaster, and in the last eight years of his life also Duke of Aquitaine, was born in 1340 and lived until 1399. Thus at his death he was quite old for someone of his generation, particularly a male engaged in warfare. Fighters of his generation rarely lived past their fiftieth birthday. Although John of Gaunt was the second surviving son of King Edward III, he inherited the Lancaster title and fabulous properties not from his father but from his father-in-law, the first Duke of Lancaster, who died in 1363.

Thereby John of Gaunt became the richest man in Western Europe who was not a crowned head (it is impossible to separate crown lands of the English and French monarchies from their personal possessions). At least three hundred lords and gentry were personally loyal, under written contracts called indentures, to the Duke of Lancaster. Gaunt had vast landholdings, especially in the north of England, and the finest house in London. He ruled over thousands of peasants.

Two of the best epic romances written between 1150 and 1400 were *Lancelot, or the Knight of the Cart,* written in northern France around 1180 by Chrétien de Troyes, and a work of unkown authorship called *Sir Gawain and the Green Knight,* written in central England around 1375. What do these works tell us about the world of John of Gaunt?

In each poem the hero pursues a perilous quest—alone, having left behind King Arthur and his Round Table. In each there are amorous adventures with beautiful women. Lancelot succumbs to the women's charms, but Gawain does not. There are also many military adventures from which Lancelot and Gawain emerge triumphant or at least get off by fighting to a draw. Both Lancelot and Gawain return in triumph to King Arthur's court. Running through both poems is a strain of sadomasochistic sexuality. There is a pronounced psychological sexual adventurism in both poems. This, along with the military adventures, is what grabbed the attention of the contemporaries who listened to these great romantic epics.

In many ways, John of Gaunt epitomized the ideals of these stories. In some ways, he surpassed them. In both *Lancelot* and *Gawain* the knights of the Round Table mount modest operations, simply described. The two knights go off on their lonely and perilous quests. In reality, John of Gaunt would travel only with many companions. The other difference in the *mise-en-scène* is that Gaunt lived in elaborate castles, such as his home base of Pontefract. He spent lavishly on décor, which was much more impressive than that of the battlements occupied by Arthur and his knights. This was the age that inaugurated the building of the elaborate French châteaus. In addition to occupying palatial mansions, the high aristocracy spent lavishly on dress and diet, and on gift-giving (especially gifts from men to women), far more so than the modest and austere world the Arthurian Round Table would allow.

Casting a dark shadow, however, was what we call the Hundred Years' War. It really began in the 1350s and '60s. That period was followed by thirty years or so of long truces. The war flared up again the second and third decades of the fifteenth century, to be followed by the ignominious expulsion of the English monarchy's forces from all but one port city in France. Joan of Arc is alleged to have played a significant role in that expulsion.

Meanwhile, for long periods, much of the western third of France was ravaged by the English lords and knights. Even when there were no military campaigns under way, the French countryside and towns were heavily affected by guerrilla warfare. Why should the lavishly living aristocracy of England and France, with so much to be grateful for, have gotten involved in this almost interminable conflict? Glory and greed are what motivated the nobles to undertake a century of intermittent warfare. For glory on the battlefield, they wanted to put on elaborate armor and show their valor, even though the cost of war was beyond the resources of the English and French monarchies.

Greed entered the picture as well. The English sought to keep the French out of the wine-growing region of Gascony

(Bordeaux). The English sought to dominate the textile-manufacturing cities of Flanders (Belgium). Past the dazzle of burnished steel there were strategic reasons for the Hundred Years' War.

Beyond the glory and greed there lay the dynastic claim of Edward III to the French crown, sheer nonsense that was taken seriously by some members of the English aristocracy, including John of Gaunt.

This was John of Gaunt's world—a society of great propertied wealth for the aristocracy, where the nobility could live very well on its income. It did so in any case, but billions of dollars were drained away in warfare. The arts and humanities, higher learning and exquisite craftsmanship played significant roles in Gaunt's world, though this culture did not fulfill its potential because a cloud of poisonous conflict hung over English and French society.

It was a world in which the Middle Ages were passing away and the Renaissance struggled to be born. Gaunt's world was one in which great achievements in literature and the arts were partly inhibited by aspirations to military glory and the dictates of greed. It was a world in transition, and Gaunt was its central figure.

⟡

The greatest British historian of the Middle Ages, Sir Richard Southern (1912–2001), in his first and most influential book, *The Making of the Middle Ages* (1953), showed that the two creative components of medieval culture and society were the Roman Catholic Church and the aristocracy. In the final chapter of *Making*, Southern portrayed the transition "from epic to romance" in the twelfth century, by which he meant that the blending of aristocracy and Church was impinging on human consciousness and was giving rise to a more emotional sensibility, which in turn led to the flowering of medieval civilization.

In his last two books, *Robert Grosseteste* (1986) and *Scholastic Humanism and the Unification of Europe* (1997), Sir Richard explored intellectual movements within the Church in the late twelfth and thirteenth centuries that followed from the integration of aristocracy and Church.

The Last Knight focuses on the other side of Southern's original polarity of Church and aristocracy. It is an attempt to explore the aristocracy of the fourteenth century through the life and times of John of Gaunt, Duke of Lancaster. Through studying Gaunt, we find that the world of the late fourteenth century at all levels of society and with regard to many facets of culture and politics opens up for us as through a prism. Gaunt was the last great aristocrat of the Middle Ages. After his death the European world begins to change in dramatic ways and history moves into the era of Renaissance or Early Modern Times.

Like the elite in all societies, including our own, Gaunt had to respond to challenges appearing on the horizon in peace and war, in politics and the economy, in religion and the arts. Studying Gaunt is an entry point to the complex world of the later Middle Ages. Knowing Gaunt allows us to understand the social and cultural structure of late medieval England, to see how components of that structure melded and functioned integrally.

The elites in all societies, whether the high aristocracy of the Middle Ages or the billionaire American capitalists of today, have to make important decisions with respect to the wealth and power they control. These decisions are heavily conditioned by family, class, and intellectual traditions. Yet the elites encounter new circumstances and novel challenges, and how they respond to these innovations is critical for social stability.

By their very nature elites tend to be conservative of prevailing institutions and ideas. But that does not mean they can avoid interacting with change or providing the means by which elements of the old world can mesh with novel trends. When elites do not perform these accommodating services, revolution is the result. When elites do their job, society makes adjustments but continues to function effectively.

☙❧

The origins of the aristocracy of which John of Gaunt was a prime exemplar go back to the period between A.D. 800 and 1000. This was the time when the short-lived empire of Charlemagne, the Carolingian empire, which embraced France, western Germany, and northern Italy, was disintegrating because of attacks from the Scandinavian Vikings to the north, the Asiatic Magyars (Hungarians) to the east, and the Muslim Arabs to the south and east.

Since the emperor of the Latin Christian world of Western Europe could no longer protect many of the lords and peasants of the West from this three-pronged invasion, they turned to more local officials, previously appointed by the Carolingian emperor, called dukes and counts. A duke was originally a local military leader; a count was a supervisor of legal matters in a locality.

By 900 the terms "duke" and "count" meant the same thing: a hereditary great landlord who exercised protection and control over a region. To the dukes and counts the ordinary lords in the region owed loyalty, promising to love what the duke or count loved and hate what the duke or count hated. In practice this meant military service, rents, and taxes owed to the duke or count. In return, as he sometimes kissed the lesser lord on the mouth (the "kiss of peace") in an elaborate ceremony, the duke or count promised to protect and help the lesser lord as his "vassal." In origin the word *vassus* meant simply "boy." The vassals were the "boys" who gathered around a duke or count and fought for him.

The vassals wore tunics of chain mail supplemented by breastplates and open-faced helmets. They learned to fight on horseback—this was made easier by the introduction of the stirrup. The duke or count was responsible for providing the vassals' armor and horse, free meals in his castle, and a place to sleep in front of the fireplace in his dining hall. He also provided unlimited amounts of beer, ale, and mead (fermented honey). The vassals were essentially companions of and fighters for the duke or count.

A grant of land from the duke or count to his vassal was often part of the deal. It was set down in an elaborate document called a charter, written on parchment (prepared sheepskin). The crux of the ceremony of vassalage was in the lesser lord kneeling before the duke or count, swearing his fealty (loyalty) and homage (obedience); then a two-handed handshake was exchanged between the duke or count on the one side and the vassal-lord on the other.

These arrangements, which lawyers later called feudal, gave the duke or count great military, legal, and political power. The obedience and loyalty of the duke or count to the Carolingian emperor became more nominal and intermittent.

By A.D. 950 the vestiges of the Carolingian empire had vanished and the dukes and counts had gained a high degree of wealth, prestige, power, and autonomy. In the eastern half of the Carolingian empire, between the Rhine and the Elbe, the dukes of Saxony in the north made claim to the imperial title. In the west, in France, the counts of Paris took the title of king. But in neither case did these titular claims interfere with the rise of the new aristocracy of hereditary dukes and counts.

In the twelfth century members of the new aristocracy had to accommodate themselves to the ambitions of French kings and German emperors. The responses of the dukes and counts varied greatly from one noble to another and from one decade to another and were heavily influenced by the personal political skills of individual monarchs.

In 1180 the German emperor's power over the dukes and counts in his territory was strongly entrenched. By 1250 the emperor's power was at best nominal. In 1150 the kings in Paris were still, in effect, only counts of the principality in and around Paris. By 1225 the Parisian kings dominated the north of France and were beginning to exercise ambitions in the south.

Meanwhile, other factors besides these political ones affected the life of the aristocracy. The spread of literacy to the courts turned the word "court" from a purely legal term to one that also had a social meaning. A code of civilized behavior developed for the aristocracy.

Another factor was the rise in the value of real estate owned by the dukes and counts. Whatever their relationship to an emperor or king, the high noble families became phenomenally wealthy, as real estate prices steadily inflated between 1150 and 1280 as the population tripled or quadrupled. The term "aristocrat" now signified a very wealthy landed person of distinguished lineage and also distinctly civilized behavior.

Severe limitations on the expansion of European aristocracies also affected political and social development. The Latin Christian elite succeeded in reconquering Iberia and Sicily from the Muslims, but attempts to establish European principalities in the eastern Mediterranean met with only partial and temporary success.

The First Crusade of 1095 gained Jerusalem and a significant part of what is today the state of Israel. None of the succeeding six Crusades was able to stave off the inexorable Muslim reconquest in the eastern Mediterranean. Fifty years after Jerusalem was taken by French crusaders in 1095, the Holy City was again in Muslim hands, and it remained so until 1917. By 1290 the last stronghold of the European aristocracy in the Middle East, the fortress of Acre on the sea in what is now northern Israel, was again taken by the Muslims.

The failure of the Crusades to establish permanent European aristocratic enclaves in the Muslim world greatly affected the politics of Western Europe between 1150 and 1450. Unable to push outward to establish colonies in the eastern Mediterranean, the kings and nobles were left to fight each other over contested lands inside Western Europe. The Germans tried to conquer northern Italy. The English and French fought over control of the western third of France.

With a renewed close attention to the history and literature of ancient Rome in the twelfth century, the medieval aristocracy saw itself mirrored in the accounts of the ancient Roman nobility. Some made doubtful claims to direct descent from the ancient Roman aristocracy. These specious historical claims were part of an effort to give clear identity to an aristocracy that was differentiating itself from the mass of ordinary knights or gentry who served as vassals of the great lords.

The historicizing ideology that harked back to Rome had little impact. What counted in the crystallization of aristocracy were more pragmatic interests, such as the grant of an inheritable title of duke or count by a Carolingian emperor, supplemented by grants of high titles by later monarchs. The holding of great tracts of land was also important, and it allowed for a degree of social mobility—very wealthy upper-middle-class gentry could sometimes gain aristocratic title. Serving as frontier chieftains on the borders of England and Scotland, or on the eastern German frontiers against the Slavs, was another route into the titular aristocracy. After 1300 such social mobility became more rare, although it was not entirely blocked off, as even merchants and bankers sometimes made their way into the entitled aristocracy.

In the fourteenth century members of the European aristocracy stressed their bloodlines as descendants of the companions of Charlemagne or some other famous king, such as William the Conqueror of England. The aristocrats, partly in response to the existence of hundreds of thousands of ambitious, socially mobile ordinary knights, saw themselves as more of a closed caste.

An emotional aura now surrounded the high aristocracy, drawing upon cultural and literary developments.

John of Gaunt stood at the very top of the European aristocracy of his day, in the late fourteenth century. His royal bloodline, his vast estates, and his ducal title defined his top-level social status. But there was something beyond his tangible and definable assets. Gaunt was Gaunt, a brand name, like Rockefeller, Murdoch, or Agnelli today.

⌒◯◯◯

Like bearers of the great capitalist names of today, Gaunt symbolized not only wealth but a particular culture. He stood for something in the world of the fourteenth century simply by being Gaunt. Therefore he is a key entry point into what the aristocracy of his day was like.

Scrutinizing Gaunt allows us to learn much not only about war and property, but also about women, entertaining, government, diet, religion, and the arts. Focusing on John of Gaunt allows us to uncover the aristocratic world at the end of the Middle Ages.

Between the late 1940s and early 1960s the American novelist John O'Hara, in a series of novels—*Ten North Frederick, From the Terrace, The Lockwood Concern*—depicted wealthy people. Although O'Hara was dealing with a class slightly below that of the top stratum of American society, he has many acute observations on how his people functioned, particularly on how the families tried to preserve their wealth and status beyond the first successful generation.

Gaunt benefited from the medieval world's mechanism for transmitting inherited wealth and power and from a considerably more static class structure than anything the modern West knows. But a few days on the campus of Princeton University—which at its core has not changed since I was a graduate student and teacher there for eight years in the 1950s—and perusal of the "Sunday Styles" section of the *New York Times* will disabuse anyone of the notion that there is an absolute difference between the very rich in the medieval world and in our own. Perhaps the changes have been greatest at the level of the working class, in that today's American billionaire capitalists find their most downtrodden and malleable workers in the factories of East Asia and Latin America, rather than in the local peasantry.

⌘

William Shakespeare, in *Richard II,* left us an impression of John of Gaunt that is indelible. (I was fortunate to see the play at Oxford in 1955, with Paul Scofield in the leading role.) Shakespeare presents Gaunt as old and doddering, but he also puts into Gaunt's mouth the most patriotic speech in the English language. To Shakespeare's Gaunt, England is "this sceptre'd isle . . . This other Eden, demi-paradise."

A second literary depiction of Gaunt is in a best-selling novel, *Katherine* (1954), by American writer Anya Seton. The lengthy novel is about Gaunt's relationship with his mistress and third wife, Catherine Swynford. Swynford comes across as a vigorous, beautiful, loving, and very intelligent woman. Gaunt comes across as a perfect knight, a gentleman, but somewhat colorless. It is obvious that Seton had in mind Clark Gable's portrayal of Rhett Butler in the 1939 film *Gone With the Wind.*

In the third volume (1962) of Thomas B. Costain's best-selling swashbuckling four-volume history of the Plantagenets, Gaunt gets short shrift: "Then there was John of Gaunt, suave, cultured, with great ambition, but lacking in the resolution that is the first of the great Plantagenet traits and thus is condemned to a rather shabby role in history." It is Gaunt's elder brother Edward the Black Prince who gets all the guts-and-glory in Costain's view. Costain artfully reinforces in this fictionalized history the image and information his readers already have about the Middle Ages.

There have been two efforts at a major scholarly biography of Gaunt in the twentieth century, both by English writers. The first, in 1904, was by Sydney Armitage-Smith, who after four hundred pages comes to a somewhat nebulous conclusion: "Gaunt remained true to the ethical standard of society as he knew it."

Anthony Goodman (1992) sees that Gaunt's "lifestyle provided one of the most notable examples of that multi-faceted conspicuous consumption characteristic of princely European families in the fourteenth century." I agree with this statement. Goodman sees Gaunt as mainly a political figure, a hard-working administrator. "He was the later medieval noble who most notably upheld royal authority."

I do not see any of these projections of Gaunt, from William Shakespeare through Anya Seton, Thomas B. Costain, Sydney Armitage-Smith, and Anthony Goodman, as wrong, even if I might quibble a bit with each portrait.

History and biography and historical fiction are imaginative presentations of points of view, shaped by the author's own frame of mind and by the social and cultural context in which the author wrote.

Mine could be called a sociological approach. It places Gaunt in the social, economic, religious, and political structures of his lifetime and seeks to suggest why these structures came into existence and how they functioned. I am also interested in eliciting Gaunt's character and personal life, which is not an easy thing to do for a medieval figure, giving the sparse nature of medieval sources.

Gaunt also inevitably comes up in the three best biographies of Geoffrey Chaucer, by Donald R. Howard (1987), Paul Strohm (1989), and Derek Pearsall (1992), but these eminent scholars cannot agree on the extent and significance of the relationship between the Duke and the poet. My account is closest to Howard's.

K. B. McFarlane's much-admired 1952 biography of John Wyclif does very little to illuminate Gaunt's relationship with the theologian and Oxford don. I have explored that relationship more closely.

There is a need for a study of Gaunt as a person and as someone involved in key aspects of the world of late-fourteenth-century England and Europe. I have tried to respond to that need, addressing lay readers and students, but drawing on the substantial research done on the era in recent years.

CHAPTER ONE

Old Europe

T O SEE HOW JOHN of Gaunt epitomized the height of the Middle Ages, the flowering of the period just prior to modernity, requires an understanding of the conditions that produced his era. The political and social system that developed in the period 800–1100 was successful in providing a structure with which security, stability, and economic growth occurred. Legal relationships by and large preceded security and economic growth. Feudalism was stable in the twelfth century because a nexus of judicial relationships provided for a degree of balance and harmony and allowed other components of medieval society and culture to develop.

Climatic conditions were favorable as well. Europeans were fortunate in that a warming trend developed between 1150 and 1280, leading to a longer growing season for cereal crops and an increased food supply.

Europeans were also lucky that their society was free from

pandemic disease in the period from the ninth century to the middle of the fourteenth.

Another factor in the rise of Europe was of the Europeans' own making. At the Church's urging they learned to keep their ambitions and aggression under control. The thirteenth century was the time of the longest era of peace before the nineteenth century. There were no major wars in Western Europe between 1214 and 1296. Widespread prosperity accompanied increasing legal order and political stability.

Then came the fourteenth century, the new age of war, disease, and colder climate.

A great American medieval historian, Joseph R. Strayer of Princeton, was fond of saying, "If Europe could survive the fourteenth century, it could survive anything." Barbara Tuchman, in her best-selling book *A Distant Mirror* (1978), likened the fourteenth century to the disastrous twentieth century.

What was this European civilization of the early fourteenth century? Part of the answer lies in how Europeans then referred to their civilization. They called it Latin Christendom. It had two international institutions: the Roman Catholic Church and the Holy Roman Empire of the German Nation, stretching from the Rhine to the Elbe.

Behind this façade of internationalism, however, lay ethnic nationalism and an intense localism. The papacy, its seat relocated from Rome to Avignon since the first decade of the fourteenth century, was under the thumb of the French monarchy. Many bishops and some abbots were as rich as the pope.

The Holy Roman Empire, founded by Frederick I, called Barbarossa, in the 1160s, was not a political entity. It had broken up into many separate states. Whoever held the title of Emperor was only as strong as his family's territorial resources allowed. He could be very strong in Bohemia (today the Czech Republic), like Charles IV, or in Austria, like the Hapsburg dynasty, but relatively weak a couple of hundred miles outside his own kingdom or duchy.

The Iberian Peninsula, once united under Roman rule, in 1300 stood divided into six principalities—five Christian and one (Granada in the southeast) Muslim. The division reflected the chaotic reconquest of Iberia from the Muslim lords between 1100 and 1300.

The three most important of the Iberian states were Aragon, on the Mediterranean; Portugal, on the west coast of the peninsula; and Castile, in the middle.

Portugal, a quiet land, is still independent of Spain and speaks a somewhat different Iberian dialect. Castile was famous for its fierce nobility, its dynastic quarrels, and the excellent wool its millions of sheep produced. It had an outlet to the sea but had done little to cultivate this advantage by 1300.

Aragon was the jewel of the peninsula. It was rich from its Mediterranean trade. Its great city of Barcelona is still by far the most beautiful in Spain. Aragon was closely tied to Sicily by trade, cuisine, and sometimes politics.

In 1300 the French Capetian monarchy centered in Paris effectively controlled 80 percent of what is today France. In

1314 the Capetian family that had ruled Paris since 987 died out and the crown passed to their Valois cousins. The sinews of royal administration and taxation, built up for a century and a half, were immediately loosened.

The early Valois kings were lazy, foolish, effete, or mad. Since the second half of the thirteenth century, princes of the royal family had been granted "appanages," quasiautonomous territories, such as Burgundy. Some of these appanaged princes, such as the Duke of Brittany, traded off their loyalty to the French Crown and temporarily allied with the English king.

By Gaunt's lifetime the Valois king in Paris controlled only the eastern two-thirds of what is today France, and that territory not very effectively because of the weakening of the bonds of royal administration. Even the burghers in Paris threatened the stability of the French monarchy. The monarchy's courtly scene was glorious, its political situation precarious for many decades.

Italy had one large political entity, the kingdom of Naples and Sicily in the south. Northern Italy was divided among city-states—Venice, Florence, Milan, Genoa, Rome, and a couple of dozen smaller and weaker ones.

The British Isles, too, were divided. The King of England ruled Wales and some of eastern Ireland, but Scotland was independent. Scotland was an impoverished country given to endless battles over the crown among the leading families. Lowland Scotland had some agriculture, but the chief factor in the Scottish economy was incessant raiding of northern English cities and ranches. The Scots were a nation of cattle

rustlers and horse thieves. There was no law north of Edin-
burgh and little below it until the English border was reached.
The Scottish Crown was propped up by funding from the
French monarchy, its traditional ally against England.

Europe was a highly fragmented political world. Latin
Christendom was an ideal culture or a linguistic block. It was
not an international political system. Furthermore, it was
lacking in a common political vision. The drive that the
mendicant friars had brought to the Church in the thirteenth
century had spent its force by the fourteenth. The Franciscans, who had charmed and persuaded Europe in the thirteenth century, were now internally divided over the issue of
poverty. The Spiritual Franciscans, the order's radical wing,
who sought solace in the poverty of the earliest church, were
condemned by the papacy as heretics.

A force for change in Western Europe was the emergence
of two highly urbanized areas, Belgium and northern Italy.
Here, as well as in London and Paris, merchant princes exercised power and influence. But except in Venice and Florence
these commercial capitalists had not yet developed a political
consciousness or a plan of public action.

In Venice and particularly Florence, merchant families
such as the Medici took over the running of government, often
competing with one another for power in a highly factious situation. As a way of establishing their identity, the merchant
families were strong supporters of scholars, philosophers,
painters, and sculptors who were fashioning a revival of classi-

cal humanism, distinguishing themselves by slowly separating from the medieval scholastic world that prevailed in the north.

What this incipient Renaissance stressed was the opening of elementary and secondary schools that taught writing in the mode of imperial Rome, 50 B.C.–A.D. 200, and the reading of the Latin literature of that era. Scholars under the patronage of the merchant families scoured the monastic, cathedral, and university libraries for better texts of Cicero, Horace, Ovid, and Virgil. In Florence Platonism became fashionable again and competed with university Aristotelianism. The long scholastic treatise was challenged by the short rhetorical essay. The more objective and naturalistic classical view of the human body was emulated by painters and sculptors.

When John of Gaunt died in 1399, this neoclassical humanism was just beginning to have an impact on English and French culture. By 1450 the impact would be highly visible.

Divisions within Christendom were not the only reason for the violence of the fourteenth century. A dark cloud looming over Latin Christendom was the Muslim Ottoman Turkish empire-sultanate in the eastern Mediterranean, including Asia Minor (the Asian part of Turkey today). The Turks bypassed besieged Constantinople, the Eastern Christian fortress on the Bosphorus—they did not take it until 1453—and had begun to penetrate the Balkans. That is how Bosnia became Muslim. In the mid-fourteenth century a group of Latin Christian nobles launched a Crusade against the Ottoman Turks to prevent their advance into Greece. In northern Greece, at Necropolis, the Turks decimated the Latin army, and Greece would be ruled by the Turks until the nineteenth century.

The Turkish army was a highly disciplined and well-armed company of mercenaries. The Turks struck fear into the hearts of the Europeans, who talked about another Crusade but did nothing. Instead, the Latin nobles joined a Crusade against the hapless pagan Wends (Slavs) in eastern Germany. In the early seventeenth century the tide of Muslim advance would reach the gates of Vienna before it was stopped with the help of a Polish king.

Poland in the late Middle Ages and in the sixteenth century was conjoined into a dual kingdom with Lithuania to form an important military and political entity. Poland became the golden land of the Jews, whose commercial, banking, and managerial skills were of great help to the monarchy and nobility.

Scandinavia was dominated by the militaristic, expansionist kingdom of Sweden and by the German commercial cities on the Baltic, like Rostock and Hamburg, that made up the autonomous Hanseatic League. The Hanseatic League built a maritime empire on the herring trade.

⟨⟨⟨⟩⟩⟩

The most effective institution in the old Europe of Latin Christendom was the university. There were a dozen universities, headed by the University of Paris. Although the majority of students were seeking to become lawyers, the most distinguished faculty, and one that comprised the most intellectual resources, was that of theology and philosophy. It demanded of students a complete mastery of the Bible; of classical philosophy, especially Aristotle; and of the canon law of the Church. It took sixteen years to get a doctorate in theology at Paris.

The weakness of the university was that it was largely cut off from the concerns of society. It had nothing to say about the economy and very little about the class system. Its most applied discipline, medicine, relied exclusively on textbooks from the ancient world. The university had no perception that its faculty might do something to increase the low agricultural yield per acre. Even political theory was a collection of bromides about good kings and tyrants.

But the university did demand of its few advanced students (there were a great many dropouts) immense learning and a very high degree of literacy in Latin, normally demonstrated in scholastic dialectical argument.

There was an intellectual base in the university for what would become the scientific revolution of the sixteenth century. There was interest and some progress in physics, but the development of the natural sciences was kept back by a limited knowledge of algebra—a deficiency that was not overcome until the sixteenth century.

Frustrated by this deficiency in mathematics, overwhelmed by the load of learning demanded of the students, by the mid-fifteenth century some Parisian masters were looking longingly at the humanistic movement in northern

Italy, which stressed a simplifying rhetoric and ethics rather than the old scholasticism.

Just as the river valleys continued to sustain the lords and peasants who had been growing grain there since 800, scholasticism continued to provide most of the intellectual fare in the late medieval university.

Medieval universities were well attended. Oxford University had 3,000 students in 1310. In 1954 the student population had increased to only 7,500, of whom 20 percent were now women (a percentage unlike that in any medieval university).

Certainly not more than 5 percent of the student body endured until receiving the doctorate in theology or philosophy. Most students dropped out earlier, having mastered enough theology, philosophy, and canon law to qualify for a position as a cathedral canon (priest or official) with a prebend (tenured endowment).

Cathedral canons had the best jobs in the late medieval church—high-paying, secure for a lifetime, only moderately burdensome, and attainable after five to ten years of university education. No wonder the ranks of the cathedral canons were full of the sons of wealthy gentry and the bastard offspring of the aristocracy.

Every era gets the cathedral it deserves. The preeminent new cathedral of the fourteenth century was the immense, ugly, ungainly, overdecorated cathedral of Cologne. Its walls were so thick that centuries later it survived Allied bombing raids in the Second World War, when every building for miles around was leveled.

The cathedral canons of Cologne were well educated and leisured. They gave little or no thought to the problems of old Europe. They lived a cloistered, segregated, and selfish life, much like Ivy League professors today.

The hardest-working people in this old Europe, except for the peasants in the field, or the textile workers of Ghent or Florence, were the bureaucrats who worked for kings, dukes, and counts. Some of them had the same university education as cathedral canons. But the majority had been trained in one of three specialized secular law schools: Bologna, in northern Italy; Montpellier, in southern France; or the Inns of Court, in London. Bologna and Montpellier taught Roman law derived directly from the codex of the sixth-century Byzantine emperor Justinian I. The Inns of Court taught a mixture of English feudal law and Roman law.

Graduates of these law schools could always find work in the expanding bureaucracies of secular government. They were paid about the same as prebendary cathedral canons, but they worked much harder, surrounded by tons of parchment, smoky candles, and pounds of sealing wax (for documents).

They were faced with three persistent problems. First, the *buzones* ("big shots," originally meaning crossbow bolts) they worked for were frequently lazy, ill, or mad, or were traveling somewhere. Second, no matter how assiduous the lawyers were in inventing, levying, and collecting taxes, they could never put together enough money to fight a protracted war. Third, they had to contend with a myriad of local loyalties, ethnicities, and dialects.

But they persisted. Historians nowadays claim that the medieval bureaucrats were engaged in something they call "state formation." The aristocrats had no use for the bureaucrats, disliked them intensely, except for those that a great landed family itself employed.

The future lay with the cathedral canons and lawyer-bureaucrats. They were signposts pointing to the rise of a professional middle class, the existence of which distinguishes the modern as opposed to the medieval world. There were plenty of merchant princes and captains of commerce about, but outside northern Italy, and especially Venice and Florence and the Hanseatic League, they were not interested in political power and leadership in society. In northern Italy and some parts of Germany, a commercial revolution with political implications had begun. Elsewhere the old world of the predominance of landed aristocrats like John of Gaunt still prevailed.

⟨༝⟩

The tectonic plates of society, moving away from the old Europe of the Middle Ages, were starting to vibrate in John of Gaunt's lifetime. This was represented not so much by the rise of merchant princes—the traders of the Hanseatic League who might handle such commodities as pickled herring, or the bourgeois nobility of Florence with their boom-and-bust banks and their art collections—as in the emergence of a new intolerance for the "others," the minorities in society.

These minorities were heretics, Jews, and gays. Previously they had been more or less ignored. Now they were subject to frequent persecution. The frustrations of the affluent peasants and lower middle class in the towns were let out against the minorities, the "others."

Early medieval society had been a tolerant one and had done nothing against separated religious communities that offered closeness and assistance under one theological banner or another. Now the separated religious communities were deemed "heretical" and were attacked by ecclesiastical officials and courts and by so-called Crusades dominated by minor nobility wanting to seize the so-called heretics' lands. This is what happened to the Albigensians in southern France in the thirteenth century. In the 1320s a zealous bishop was still pursuing them in the foothills of the Pyrenees, to which they had retreated.

There was a time, between 800 and 1100, when Jews (of whom there were 1.5 million in Christian Europe) were protected by kings and princes because of the commercial and banking services they provided. Occasionally a Christian scholar would even seek dialogue with Talmudic rabbis, drawing upon the latters' Biblical learning. No longer. By 1300 the Jews were subject to persecution and exile. They were regarded as Christ-killers who engaged in the ritual slaughter of Christian children.

The Jews were excluded from England and most of

France around 1300 and were the victims of pogroms in Iberia. The Jews were reduced to hazardous living in the Holy Roman Empire, seeking out princes or bishops who would give them temporary refuge and experiencing an enormous decline in wealth. Many rabbis retreated into a mystical and astrological world called the Kabbalah. Around 1500 the Jews found security and renewed prosperity in Poland.

The canon law of the Church contained prohibitions against sodomy, which included homosexual relations. But these were ignored until the thirteenth century. King William II of England, called William Rufus (r. 1087–1100), was openly gay and never married. In the same era an archbishop of Canterbury who was a prominent theologian cultivated a group of gay young monks in his cathedral. By contrast, when English kings in the fourteenth century were openly gay, they were forced to abdicate and were then killed, as was the fate of Edward II and Richard II.

There was a maniacal shift against gays after 1200. It was part of the intolerance of what was now a persecuting society. This intolerance toward "others" reflected the new feeling of collective action on the part of the lower middle class and the upper stratum of the working class. Intolerance and persecution were the outlets for their anger, envy, and insecurity. The high aristocracy rarely participated in the new intolerance.

The intolerance toward minorities of Jews, gays, and heretics was reflective of an expanding urban environment. The thirteenth century was an age of expansion of towns and cities. The urban environment was intensely competitive economically. Accosting anyone who could be suppressed, disfranchised, or expelled on grounds of being an "other" was a way of reducing the pressure. This persecution was often carried out at the behest of Franciscan or Dominican friars, who sought to gain the loyalty of the urban working class and lower middle class by cultivating their prejudices.

Medieval towns were physically crowded, medically unhealthy, and poorly sanitized sites that fostered anger, jealousy, and paranoia. The streets were replete with underemployed, unemployed, and ruthlessly exploited young men ready to demonstrate and riot over almost any political or religious issue.

John of Gaunt and some other aristocrats were often the object of the fury from the streets. Gaunt had to be very cautious in the tempestuous Parliament of 1376. In Paris, Ghent, Bruges, and Florence the noise and fury from the streets sometimes coalesced into revolutionary movements.

That never happened in London in the Middle Ages, but seething resentment in the streets was a continuing threat and would sometimes boil over into riots.

Old Europe in 1340, the year John of Gaunt was born, was an unfinished civilization. It would have been hard for any contemporary to predict where Europe was going.

The great promise of the long peace and prosperity of the

thirteenth century had ended. The business cycle was heading downward and Europe would not enter another era of persistent prosperity until the sixteenth century, when silver and gold from the Americas and the discovery of gold mines in central Europe inflated the money supply. Europe, so fortunate in its climate since the tenth century, now experienced much more frigid conditions and shorter growing seasons. Pandemics spread by cattle and rats threatened the stability and strength of the population.

Above all lurked the constant threat of the Muslim Turks advancing through the Balkans, coupled with the inability of the medieval Western states to organize an effective counterattack. The future of Latin Christian civilization seemed perilous.

Once Roman armies had vanquished both the barbarian Arabs and the heathen Germans. Now that seemed like a forgotten dream. Once Alexander the Great, in the 320s B.C., had marched with fifty thousand faithful companions eastward through central Asia and into northern India. Now that seemed only a poetic fantasy.

Once, long ago, Europe had stood for strength, ambition, victory. Now such aggressive tracks were covered by the dust of centuries, and the roads that had proudly supported Alexander's and Caesar's armies were covered by sand and mud.

There were, however, three factors militating in favor of European survival. The first was the immensely rich legacy of ancient Rome and Greece, now being cultivated more deeply in

Europe. The classical world's achievements in philosophy, science, and literature were again laid bare by scholars. The merchants and bankers of northern Italy were prepared to fund research into a deeper understanding of the classical world, a recovery of the culture of Athens and Rome that had given Europeans confidence in themselves during their better days.

The second factor in Europe's favor as it confusedly faced the indomitable Muslim Turks was the wealth and commercial enterprise of the northern Italian cities whose commercial companies and banks bulged with the cash to counter economic depression, cold, and disease and begin the transformation of the European economy into something structurally resembling capitalism. Italian merchants like Marco Polo followed the silk routes eastward through the dust and turmoil of Central Asia to China. (Among other benefits the Italian voyagers got from the Chinese was the idea of making pasta, a cheap and nutritious cereal food that improved the Italian diet.)

The third positive element in European life, one that provided prospective leadership against the Muslim threat and reinvigorated politics and society, were the scions of the great aristocratic families. They were lucky that the Muslim threat never got farther west than the gates of Vienna, as this gave the aristocracy a time to breathe and to cultivate a distinctive way of life. John of Gaunt, leader of one of the most prominent families in Europe, never had to go crusading. He could fight other battles, as well as take on more subtle struggles within a changing England.

CHAPTER TWO

The Great Families

JOHN OF GAUNT belonged to a family that was as proud of its lineage as any in Europe. Only the French kings could express such confidence in their blue-blooded quality. Gaunt was the son of the long-lived Edward III and younger brother of the most glorious knight in Christendom, Edward the Black Prince.

In the early fourteenth century, three hundred or so families constituted the high aristocracy of Western Europe. Within each country the families preferred to intermarry among themselves, but occasionally the marriages took place on an international scale. Some of these international marriages undertaken for diplomatic and economic reasons turned out well. Some were disasters from the start.

King Edward II's marriage to the French princess Isabella, the "She-Wolf of France," produced endless misery on both sides. The marriage of King Richard II to Anne of Bohemia was probably never consummated. The marriage of

John of Gaunt to Constance of Castile was an unhappy one; eventually he abandoned her.

The males of the great families held sonorous noble titles. The women were usually married by eighteen or went into a nunnery. The women were breeders of the next generation among the great families and perhaps a third of the time they were dead by the age of thirty, exhausted by bearing children or struck down in the roulette of childbirth in an age of unscientific obstetrics. Yet there were women of the great families, chiefly widows, who lasted into their fifties or later.

Because of the high and early mortality among the married women of the great families, the males pursued serial marriages, one young bride replacing another who had just died. At least two marriages were common for the aristocratic male; three or four marriages quite frequent. In addition, the males of the high aristocracy tended to have many mistresses and to produce droves of bastard children, who were usually taken care of in a very modest way, but were sometimes supported almost as lavishly as the legitimate progeny.

The greater part of the wealth of the great families came from inherited estates worked by peasants under various contractual arrangements. No one could aspire to any status among the great families without a landed income of at least several million dollars a year. Without the vast landed income, aristocrats could not maintain their lavish lifestyle, participate in politics and war, entertain other scions of the great families at lavish feasts and elaborate tournaments, or be patrons of musicians and painters, collect beautifully hand-illustrated books, or commission sculptures (usually commissioned for their graves and mausoleums in cathedrals).

It is not easy to provide equivalence between medieval and modern money. But it is safe to say that in 1370 Gaunt's family controlled more than $5 billion in annual rents. The Plantagenets and their successors, the Lancastrians, owned land all over the country but principally in the northern half of England, the land of sheep and cattle ranges.

The members of the great families were literate, but in vernacular languages, rarely in the Latin that made you officially literate and involved many years of study at a university. The great families did not educate their sons at universities unless one of them was chosen to become a bishop, or even a cardinal or pope. Even as late as the mid-twentieth century, the educational level of the great European aristocratic families had not changed much. Charles, Prince of Wales (b. 1948), was the first member of the English royal family to get a university degree.

The great families employed lawyers, accountants, and secretaries to manage their incomes and estates, as well as supervisors to keep the peasants in line. The great families almost never were in the direct presence of a peasant. They had little in the way of common experiences or even common language with the working class. The international common language of the great families was French, a situation that still prevailed in the eighteenth century and to a large extent does so today, although now English would also be mastered.

French was the first Romance language to attain clarity in grammar and vocabulary. It was also the preferred language of courtiers. In the twelfth century, great literature was already being written in French.

On the lands of the great families there were frequently towns, which were commercial centers whose markets would be licensed and taxed by the lord on whose land the town was built. The high aristocrat would have formal, ceremonial dealings with the mayor and the town council. He would do business with the bankers in the towns, frequently running up huge debts to them. Even someone as wealthy as Gaunt took some loans from bankers. In 1200 most of these bankers were Jews. By 1325 most were either Italians or locals.

A group of about three hundred Jewish families from Rouen followed William the Conqueror to England in the late eleventh century. A century later about ten of these families were very wealthy and were engaged in large-scale banking for the great aristocratic families.

The decline of the Jewish bankers went through three stages. First, the size of loans some aristocrats demanded stretched the resources of the Jewish bankers. The commitment of huge sums was too risky.

Second, after about 1175 the English government levied such heavy tallages (direct taxes) on the Jews that the bankers' liquidity was sharply reduced. For every pound the

Jewish bankers were making on their loans to aristocrats, at least half was destined in taxes for the royal treasury. The income from Jewish sources was now so important to the Crown that a special branch of the Exchequer, the accounting division of the royal treasury, had to be set up to squeeze Jewish taxpayers.

Third, the coming of the Franciscan friars to England in the 1230s signaled a new era of Christian Judeophobia. Jews as Christ-killers was a favorite theme of Franciscan sermons, delivered in the vernacular to middle-class and peasant audiences, inciting them to pogroms.

By 1250 the great Florentine banking houses such as the Peruzzi and the Frescobaldi were at work in London, York, and Lincoln, willing and able to service the high aristocracy with huge loans. But the economic condition of the Jewish population in England (numbering some five thousand people) went into sharp decline even before Edward I expelled them in 1290. Many of them ended up in the Rhineland, and from there their descendants migrated to their golden land, Poland.

Outside of northern Italy and the Low Countries the great families had nothing to do with industrial production except as consumers of luxury goods—jewels, tapestries, and fine clothes. The great families were the main consumers of these finely crafted luxury items. Even into the nineteenth and twentieth centuries, the high aristocracy had very little to do with the "trades."

The great families in England always stood in a close but

tense relationship with the royal family. They were often related to the royals by birth (younger sons, cousins) or marriage. Kings needed their prowess in war and their political skills, but the royals were wary of the ambition of a great family to take the throne.

This competition led to unseemly squabbles, exiles, and murders. Such dark episodes were accepted as a normal part of the life of a great family. Today a billionaire, tomorrow an impoverished exile (if not a victim of assassination), then in a few years possibly returned by the Crown to one's previous station and wealth. Henry IV, Gaunt's son, learned to endure such deprivations. Gaunt did not come to his son's aid. He knew that Henry would bounce back.

Besides the royal family, the other institution competing with the great families was the Catholic Church, even though some ecclesiastical officials were themselves from high aristocratic background and had been given the long and expensive Latinate university education to allow them to rise to prominence in the Church.

In the period 800–1200 there was a close alliance between the Church and the great families. The high aristocracy endowed the Church with land and the churchmen unequivocally supported the authority of the great families over the other social classes. Through the sacramental and penitential system, the ecclesiastics assured the lords that their passage through Purgatory into Heaven would be rapid and comfortable.

By the fourteenth century the long-established alliance between the great families and the Church was eroding. The high aristocracy no longer provided the Church with new rich landed endowments, only very small token ones. The aristocrats chose to preserve their property for their children, legitimate and illegitimate. Nor could the great lords maintain their high standard of living if they continued to give away significant wealth to the Church.

Furthermore, in the thirteenth century there had emerged for the first time in medieval Europe, among the friars and university teachers, intimations of a more radical and egalitarian social philosophy. A close reading of the Gospels indicated that Jesus and his initial followers were poor people. From this it followed that there was something intrinsically good and holy about the status of poverty.

From there, radical thinking among the Franciscans raised the question of why there was such a polarity in the social distribution of wealth. If poverty was holy, what was the moral and theological significance of wealth, including landed, inherited wealth? The great families found these egalitarian glimmerings discomfiting. Gaunt would patronize radical thinking, but not of this stripe.

ᕮᘏᘏᘏᕤ

In the nineteenth century German and French medievalists worried about the origins of the great families. Did the great families descend from the provincial aristocracy of the

Roman empire or from the barbarian chieftains who invaded the Roman empire between 400 and 600? Did they originate in the Latin or the Germanic world? Both, it seems. Rarely can one of the great families be traced back earlier than the period 800–1000, the period of the great Carolingian empire and its breakup into constituent kingdoms and duchies.

By 1200 the great families had embraced a code of civilized conduct called chivalry (which originally meant horsemanship) or courtliness. This involved treating women of the upper class decently (confining rapes to peasant women), genteel consideration and respect for other nobles, a certain elegance in dress and restraint in behavior at the table, and elaborate rituals of romantic love.

Sons of the great families still died on the battlefield, but by 1300, lords captured in war were more often held in comfortable captivity until they were ransomed by their families. It was the peasants who were slaughtered in the Hundred Years' War.

John of Gaunt was a direct descendant of a heathen Scandinavian chieftain named Rollo. In 911 Rollo with his Viking band seized a piece of the faltering Carolingian empire in northern France, roughly coterminous with the old archdiocese of Rouen, and transformed it into the Duchy of Normandy.

Among Rollo's successors, who were converted to Christianity and civilized by the Church, the most politically skillful was William the Bastard (later the Conqueror). He organized his personal and property arrangements with the duchy's nobility so as to create a very strong army of a thousand cavalrymen. With additional assistance from mercenaries recruited from other parts of northern France, William invaded and seized England in 1066 and settled his French followers on lands taken from the less bellicose and less militarily skillful English lords.

In the middle of the twelfth century the Conqueror's family became joined in marriage with another great family from northern France, the Plantagenets. In the next 150 years the Plantagenet dynasty and its well-trained officials showed remarkable innovative capacity to develop taxation and legal systems and representative government. The founder of the dynasty, Henry II (r. 1154–1189), along with his French wife, Eleanor of Aquitaine, also showed sympathy with the developing ideals of chivalry and courtliness and with patronage of the arts.

The emblem of the Plantagenet dynasty was three yellow leopards. It still was in the time of John of Gaunt. The distinctive Lancastrian branch of the family that John of Gaunt founded, which sat on the English throne from 1399 to 1471, added in the fifteenth century as its personal emblem a red rose.

◦✠◦

The members of the great families did not like to be alone. They traveled and dined with companions drawn from noble families. They always were accompanied by an armed body-guard of at least a half-dozen mounted soldiers, called knights. When he sat down to dinner, a great lord like John of Gaunt would ordinarily be joined by at least two dozen people—his family, aristocratic companions, some of his armed bodyguard, and a churchman or two.

At least once a month, to demonstrate his wealth, status, and power, a lord like Gaunt would hold a banquet with between three hundred and five hundred people attending, including the smaller landholders of the county, other great lords and their entourages, several bishops and abbots, and even an itinerant royal judge or tax collector. Musicians and minstrels would play and sing on a balcony overlooking the dining hall, illuminated by hundreds of candles, which perpetually threatened a fire.

To implement such a feast required hundreds of servants. The food would take days to prepare. The kitchen was in a separate building or in a separate wing of the main building, and puffing waiters would rush to bring in the food on huge trays before it got cold. The food was basically barbecues and roasts supplemented by salted or pickled fish and huge meat pies. Red Bordeaux wine as well as beer and cider were served in endless portions. Dessert consisted of custards washed down with sweet wines.

The only eating utensil before the fifteenth century was a knife. All the banqueters ate with their hands and wiped their greasy fingers on towels provided by servants, or often on their own clothes—which, along with being questionable personal hygiene, must have made for an odoriferous dining hall.

Members of the great families lived in drafty castles surrounded by high walls and deep moats. By the fourteenth century the great lords were building country houses that were less military and more commodious. Until the thirteenth century private bedrooms were at a premium; they were inhabited by the lord and his wife and a few prominent guests. In such a house in 1300, dozens of knights still slept on furs or mats on the floor in front of great fires in the main banquet hall. By 1400 there were enough private rooms to accommodate dozens of guests. The servants slept in attics and basements.

A privilege of being a member of a great family was the use of a wooden privy built over the castle moat. In 1200 the less privileged would urinate and defecate in the courtyard. But writers of books on courtliness reminded the great lords like Gaunt to try to have sufficient privies for use by all guests. By the time Gaunt died in 1399, this comfort was probably available in at least his grander houses. Only the great lord himself was permitted to urinate inside his own dining hall, but Gaunt rarely availed himself of this ancient privilege.

In the cold and wet weather of an English winter, the only heat was provided by open fires that servants had to keep feeding and stoking.

All castles and country houses were accompanied by

barns for horses, the only means of long-distance transportation. The horses, especially if cross-bred with Arabic strains, were prized and were costly.

All this may seem a rather barbaric way to live. But very wealthy people of the landed classes were still living this way in England in the 1880s or even the 1920s. They had plenty of forks by then and occasionally a French chef would prepare more delicate cuisine. But in 1920 a privy for each guest would still have been unusual.

Many centuries earlier, bishops had been chosen by the townspeople, and abbots by their monastic communities. In the England of John of Gaunt the bishops were chosen by the great family that predominated in a county, with the assent of the royal government. Archbishops were always chosen by the Crown, as were the abbots of the older and larger monasteries, which over time had become immensely wealthy land corporations.

There was a static feeling to life among the great families. Their behavior and values were set out for them by traditional and familial customs, as in very rich American families today. All males in the great family were trained in the arts of war. By 1250 this meant the ability to fight on horseback wearing fifty pounds of plate armor. Some were skilled in hand-to-hand fighting on foot, but there was less opportunity for this Roman style of warfare than a hundred years before because now all nobility at the beginning of a battle had to fight with long lances from horseback. Again, droves of servants were needed to equip and prepare a lord for battle.

Development of skills in armored horseback fighting required years of training from the age of five and constant practice at tournaments. At these popular and expensive events, armored knights would charge at each other while passing a list, a low wooden barricade. No one was supposed to get killed in tournaments; the lances were supposed to be blunted and therefore not capable of penetrating plate armor. But lords and knights did sometimes get wounded or even killed in tournaments, often by a blow to the throat or neck just below the helmet.

The tournaments used up a lot of expensive horses. By 1350 horses in tournaments were usually armored, but this made them slow and unmanageable.

By the late fourteenth century very prominent and wealthy men like Gaunt would have special ceremonial armor to wear at tournaments, often imported from Germany or Switzerland. Ceremonial armor was especially beautiful and ornate; examples can be seen today in the Metropolitan Museum of Art in New York and the British Museum in London. Such armor was often heavier then battle-ready armor plate and further reduced mobility. But once an accoutered knight charging in the lists was unseated, that engagement was over. Knights did not engage on foot in hand-to-hand combat with swords at tournaments—that was too risky of human life.

Ceremonial armor allowed for the use of all sorts of fancy helmets and armor plating that embraced even the feet. What was almost as important as the armor itself in protecting the armored knight on horseback was a padded flap jacket that the knight wore under his armor.

In the three centuries after 1700, with the growth in the size of armies, armor was deemed too expensive for soldiers. Besides, armored soldiers were more vulnerable now than in the Middle Ages; a musket ball or a rifle bullet could penetrate armor if the gun was fired close-up. Lack of armor contributed to the tremendous casualty rates of battles in the Napoleonic wars, the American Civil War, and the two world wars. Very recently, partial armor over flap jackets has again come to be used in the American and British armies and in civilian SWAT teams.

Historians and filmmakers have had much fun depicting medieval armored knights as being so immobile as to have to be lifted into the saddle with a winch. Knights have also been depicted as being immobile after being dehorsed, weighed down by their armor. But recent practical tests by armor museums have shown that late-medieval warriors wearing plate armor were remarkably mobile, such was the skill in construction. The accouterment involved mobile chain mail, not plate armor, under the armpits, so the knights could raise their arms and mount their horses freely, with some assistance from a groom perhaps, and once dehorsed and on foot they could engage in hand-to-hand combat.

Among the aristocracy and the wealthier gentry, tournaments, which lasted from three to ten days, were grand occasions for socializing and feasting. Lords pitched elaborate tents and competed with one another to offer the most sensational picnics. As outside an American football stadium today, the barbecue pits were busy.

Women of the upper classes attended tournaments and sat in wooden bleachers on the side, along with kings and nobles too old to fight. Chivalric literature is full of stories of the ladies picking favorites among the participating knights, who might charge into the lists with a lance that bore a lady's silk handkerchief. In the more sensational chivalric poems—as in some of the poems of Chrétien de Troyes, written in the late twelfth century—a victorious knight would be rewarded with his lady's sexual favors.

What if a male member of a great family disliked or was physically or temperamentally incapable of this bellicose lifestyle? Sometimes he just suffered in silence and tried to keep out of harm's way. Sometimes he departed for years on a Crusade to the Middle East, where he usually could avoid fighting. Sometimes his family gave him a Latinate education at the university and this education prepared him to become a bishop. Seldom—but it happened—the aristocrat fled from the noble's lifestyle to become a monk.

In the thirteenth and fourteenth centuries, there was a novel alternative to a life of endless fighting and feasting: becoming a high-level royal bureaucrat. But this job required hard work around the clock, and rarely did a great lord want to stick to the drudgery of administration. Instead he might wander off to his country house and his hunting lodge. The king generally found members of the rural middle class, the gentry, much better for the constant pressure of royal service.

Great lords became royal councillors who advised the king on weighty matters, but even this privileged activity the members of the great families often found boring, and they wandered off to pursue their accustomed lifestyle of tournaments, hunting, and feasting.

The Plantagenets were not without feeling. They were conventionally pious and they were patrons of the arts. They were a close family, with deep feelings for one another. They were circumscribed in the behavior and values of their family, but they had no pity for peasants or the poor in general. Those social groups were beyond the perimeter of their empathy and sensibility.

This was the culture of domination the Plantagenets communicated to the world, and it is still common among the rich and powerful.

CHAPTER THREE

Plantagenet England

A S WAS THE CASE with all medieval royal families, and indeed has been with the great families in general, the degree to which individual Plantagenet kings were seen as strong and successful or foolish and weak varied greatly. One reason was that the knowledge of obstetrics and gynecology in the Middle Ages was rudimentary, resulting in the possibility of brain damage to the royal infants. The future kings were often raised in a very slovenly manner, and very young princes were mistakenly treated as adults. Of the Plantagenet kings, John (r. 1199–1216) was a severe manic depressive, and Edward III (r. 1327–1377) was a weakling and a coward, lacking self-confidence. Richard II (r. 1377–1399), as well as Edward II (r. 1307–1327), preferred young men over women, which aroused the nobility against them. Therefore it is not surprising that after Henry II, the founder of John of Gaunt's dynasty, among the Plantagenets only two kings before 1377 were regarded by contemporaries (and have been by most modern historians) as being strong and successful. Fortunately for England, Edward I (r. 1272–1307) and Edward III (r. 1327–1377) had very long reigns—although in the case of Edward III the reign turned out to be be too long, because in his later years he suffered bad health and dementia.

But Edward I and Edward III in his prime were not without major flaws, notably the tendency to use the country's wealth and superior institutions for adventuresome wars that were beyond even their substantial resources, thereby producing strains on the political and taxation systems.

Edward I conquered Wales, which brought no additional wealth to his kingdom; there was not a strong market for coal until the end of the fifteenth century. He also intervened in a dynastic dispute in Scotland and tried to conquer the country; he failed, leaving a mess for his incompetent successor. Finally, in 1297, Edward I got into an expensive and doubtful war with the French monarchy; he didn't achieve anything in this venture either.

By the time of Edward I, the Plantagenets had lost most of their ancestral family domains in France. They held only a small strip, never more than a hundred miles wide, that ran along the West coast of France from Bordeaux to the Pyrenees. This territory was called Gascony. Edward I had his eyes on the industrial powerhouse in the north, Flanders, and expansion of the wine-growing area along the eastern border of Gascony. He was unsuccessful.

Edward III, Gaunt's father, revived this imperialist push, launching the Hundred Years' War, Gaunt's war. In the first twenty years of the Hundred Years' War, Edward III's armies were victorious, but not enough to take Paris, which the English king now also claimed. For the rest of his reign Edward III made no headway against the French king, but his armies laid waste to much of the western third of France, becoming a curse on the French peasantry.

Edward I financed his wars by getting consent to heavy taxation through the representation of the landed and moneyed classes in Parliament. Edward III did the same in his early years, but this approach did not yield enough to support his grandiose ambitions. He resorted to taking huge loans from Italian bankers and then defaulted on the loans. In the last decade of his reign, old Edward III's government suffered severe fiscal stringency. John of Gaunt would have to use some of his abundant personal resources for his campaigns in France and Spain.

Of the early Plantagenet kings who followed Henry II, none was as effective as the two great Edwards. Henry II was succeeded by his eldest surviving sons, Richard I the Lion-Hearted (r. 1189–1199) and John. The most influential Hollywood film about medieval England, *The Adventures of Robin Hood* (1938), has stamped indelibly in the popular mind the picture of Richard the Lion-Hearted as the hero and John as the villain. The real story is more complex.

Richard was six feet two inches tall—a giant in a society

where very few men were taller than five feet five inches. Richard was a mean bully who got into noisy quarrels with people of his own social standing. He spent much of his reign on a Crusade in the Middle East, where he accomplished nothing and was held for ransom by the German emperor. He spent only a year of his reign in England and was unable to focus on the business of governance. Although Richard married, he was homosexual and had no issue.

King John was all business and showed himself to be an unusually skillful administrator, especially in financial matters. Unfortunately he was also paranoid and manic-depressive. He constantly suspected the great families of disloyalty, until they actually did rebel in 1215 and forced him to put his seal to a reform program called the Magna Carta. In one of his depressive periods (1204–1206), John, putting up very little resistance, allowed his enemy the King of France to conquer the Plantagenet ancestral lands in northern France.

Henry III (r. 1216–1272) was pious but weak and confused. He was pushed around by his brother-in-law, the King of France, and some of the great aristocratic English families. Finally, in Henry's later years, his son, the future Edward I, took over and reestablished political stability.

Edward II was a bisexual, married to a fierce French princess. He spent his time losing Scotland, cultivating his male French lovers, and getting overthrown in a palace coup launched by the Queen and her aristocratic lover. He was later murdered.

Edward III (r. 1327–1377) was a good-humored man ever trying to give his many sons and daughters a helping hand. He arranged John of Gaunt's marriage with the Duchess of Lancaster. On the battlefield Edward III was forever seeking military glory. He had no empathy whatsoever with the peasants and the poor. He was totally devoted to his family and their advancement.

It made a difference who was king of England in Plantagenet times. The king was, in effect, his own prime minister; therefore, the government could become unwound during the reign of a weak and foolish king. But there was an underside to the rule of even the supposedly strong and successful kings; they got involved in foreign wars and drained the royal treasury. Glory did not necessarily mean royal prosperity and stable government.

No one is going to understand the development of Plantagenet England by focusing on the doings of this motley collection of monarchs, even though we know a lot about them due to the thickness of government records and the anecdotes and gossip circulated by monastic and courtly writers. The dynamics of Plantagenet England lie more in the economic and cultural spheres than in the political sphere.

There are three models of economic development in medieval England. The first is the demographic model: the rise and decline of the population level affected everything else. The second model is the Marxist one: the struggle of the serf peasantry for freedom was key. The third and recent model reverts to an idea popular among historians around 1900: commercial markets and the growth of cities was central. It is possible to overlap these three models and also include cultural and religious history as affecting the development of Plantagenet England.

The lay of the land and its exploitation, the rural and urban entrepreneurial classes, the entrenchment of a parish system and the coming of the friars, the rise of the universities and the growth of literacy and learning, the spread of chivalry and courtliness among the nobility: these were the forces that stimulated and shaped Plantagenet England and made it by medieval or even modern standards a relatively prosperous and progressive society.

The population of England in 1066 was 1 million people. By 1300 it was approaching 6 million people because of the expanding food supply resulting from benign weather. Then, because of famine, disease, and economic problems in the fourteenth century as well as deteriorating climatic conditions and a shorter growing season, the population sank to 3 million people and did not again reach 6 million until the middle of the eighteenth century.

The glory of England lay not in its kings but in its lands. The central part of the country was the best grain-growing area of Europe alongside the black-earth country of the Ukraine, which was not exploited until the sixteenth century. The northern third of England was not suitable for intensive agriculture but its verdant hills and quiet valleys offered rich pasturage for sheep and cattle, which flourished in enormous numbers.

By 1250 there were probably 10 million sheep in England. They provided the best raw wool in Western Europe, mutton for a carnivorous population, and skins that were stretched and bleached to become parchment, which was the prime writing surface before the late fifteenth century.

The raw wool was exported to the cloth-weaving towns of Flanders, and from there much of it went to Florence to be further refined. The people who benefited from the wool trade comprised all classes of society: the great families who held at least a third of the land; the lesser nobility, or gentry, who along with the monastic order of the Cistercians held the rest of it in the north; the merchants in the towns; and the hardy, well-fed peasants.

In 1100 there was a lot of underdeveloped land in the great central grain-growing region (called "champaign" country in the Middle Ages). By 1250 it had been fully developed; there was a shortage of land for the gentry and peasant families; and real estate prices skyrocketed. Given that the yield per acre in the thirteenth century was very modest by modern standards, the product of the plowlands of central and south-central England was just sufficient to maintain the nutrition of a rapidly expanding population.

Since the great families held perhaps a third of the grain-growing land as their private domains, they benefited enormously from the rural inflation. It allowed them to cultivate their now extravagant lifestyle and meddle in national politics.

In 1300 in England, 85 percent of the population lived on the land. There was, however, a growing urban population; the numbers living and working in urban areas ranged from five hundred people to ten thousand (York) to sixty thousand (London).

The great merchants were engaged in exporting wool to Flanders and importing wine ("claret") from Bordeaux. But there were also thousands of local traders selling grain, meat, fish, writing materials, clothing, and shoes. Every town had its public market. The craftspeople were organized in guilds, which provided welfare services and entertainment for the middle class and working class in the towns and tried to set prices, wages, and standards of manufacture.

In the fourteenth century England began to develop its own cloth making, although exports of immense bales of raw wool to the Continent continued. The cloth industry was organized according to the putting-out, or domestic, system. Representatives of the great entrepreneurs supplied peasants with looms for their houses, and raw wool, and every few weeks went out to pick up the cloth, pay the workers, and provide new materials.

Many of the larger towns were "cities," that is, episcopal centers; the town developed around the cathedral. In the fourteenth century these ecclesiastical centers were still important. For example, Lincoln was still one of the largest half-dozen towns in the country. The cathedral clergy and other church officials were an important part of the population of these ecclesiastical towns and in some instances stimulated the burghers to become voluble and politically active.

Whether a town was ecclesiastical or secular, the burghers were in the ruling class (about 10 percent of the population), people to be reckoned with. Gaunt was probably afraid of them because they could get angry and unruly. He was certainly cautious and perplexed in their presence. Furthermore, their grants of taxes were important.

The burghers represented in Parliament (so the king could tax them more effectively) had ideas and opinions, and once in a while they expressed them. Most of the time, however, they kept quiet and followed the leadership of the gentry with whom they were compacted into a corporate House of Commons after 1340. The gentry and wealthy merchants made up the House of Commons; the nobility the House of Lords.

In London and three or four other towns there was a politics of the street—demonstrations and riots among the lower middle class. This could bother the king and the royal officials and some of the great families, including that of John of Gaunt.

In both urban and rural areas a strong push for stability and countering of political activism followed the entrenchment of the parish system. Every village had a church and a resident priest, usually paid for by a lord. London was a city of a thousand churches.

The priests generally reinforced hierarchy and fostered submission. They encouraged reliance on Church formulas and rituals to stave off medical and other misfortunes. Faith healing was a central part of religion, for the magnates, gentry, and burghers, and especially for the peasants. Reliance on faith healing normally kept the peasants quiet and contented in spite of epidemics and inadequate public health facilities.

A contrary, more radically active impulse in society resulted from the coming of the immensely popular Franciscan friars into England in the 1230s. They preached in the vernacular and often outdoors. They too propagated belief in faith healing and preached submission to ecclesiastical and secular authorities, but once in a while their sermons carried a trace of social criticism and class discontent.

In the century after 1150 there was an immense growth in literacy in the vernacular among the aristocracy, the gentry, and the merchant class due to elementary schools provided by towns and the Church. The Franciscans adopted Oxford University and made it into a prime center of Latinate learning and theological, philosophical, and scientific speculation. By 1300 radical thinking about church organization also appeared among a small minority of the friars teaching and studying in the universities.

Another aspect of cultural change deeply affected the behavior and consciousness of the great families and sometimes the upper stratum, at least, of the gentry class. This was the code of chivalry, or courtliness, which was brought to

England from France in the reign of Henry II (in the 1160s and '70s) by Queen Eleanor of Aquitaine and her hangers-on, including clerics at her court.

Chivalry posited more civilized behavior and a gloss of gentility for the high aristocracy. Aristocrats were to dress well; practice good table manners; participate in tournaments, for which the lords were to accouter themselves in special ornamental armor; take care to improve the bloodlines of their women, horses, and falcons; and be patrons of the arts. They were to treat each other, even on real battlefields, with at least a modicum of care and reciprocity.

Certainly by the early fourteenth century this code of chivalry was well entrenched among the great nobles and some of the wealthier gentry. But it was on relationships between the sexes that chivalry had perhaps its most profound social effect. Women of the upper classes must not be raped or physically abused. They could, however, be seduced.

Marriage could legitimately involve romantic love as well as property and diplomatic arrangements. But marriage vows did not preclude elaborate and ritualized forms of adultery, referred to as courtly love.

Chivalry no doubt improved the treatment of women within noble and gentry families. It also permitted promiscuity. It even gave legitimacy, in high social circles, to homoerotic relationships, which increasingly were condemned by the established Church and the more conservative ecclesiastics.

Chivalry thus included within its makeup a kind of sexual liberation. Sexual relationships among members of the great families and some of the wealthier gentry were seen as a coded mélange of connoisseurship and gamesmanship as much as were tournament jousting and falconry.

This more liberated sexual consciousness is reflected in two literary developments: close description of young women's physical attributes and elaborate inquiries into the psychology of romantic love, with all its passions and problems.

All aspects of the chivalric code and behavior pattern, save that of homoeroticism, were exemplified in the life of John of Gaunt. Along with hosting, feasting, hunting and jousting, expensive clothes, elaborate housing, and a certain civility and restraint in public behavior, there was in John's case the libido and love angle.

John of Gaunt had many mistresses; that was nothing new among the nobility. But Gaunt treated his favorite mistress with dignity and generosity and ended up marrying her and legitimating their bastard children, an action that was to have far-reaching effects on English politics and even the royal family.

English society in the late fourteenth century was liberal about heterosexual relationships and progressive on treatment of women in the upper and middle classes. But the savage hostility to the "other" that marked continental Europe in the thirteenth century had now penetrated the English kingdom.

Jews had been expelled from England in 1290, after

wave upon wave of pogroms. By Gaunt's lifetime the Anglo-Jewish families were in Germany, for the most part, on their way to Poland. In the late fourteenth century a heretical movement among the English clergy appeared, to be ruthlessly hunted down and persecuted in the fifteenth century, although never entirely obliterated. The rising hostility toward homosexuals played a part not only in the downfall of Edward II but also in ending the reign of Gaunt's nephew Richard II (r. 1377–1399).

CRRRRO

England in the middle of the fourteenth century was a boisterous, violent, and crime-ridden place. Radical fluctuations in the land market and the supply of labor exacerbated an already class-polarized, disease-ridden society. Demobilized mercenaries from the wars in France roamed the English countryside in organized gangs—this was the grim social reality behind the Robin Hood legend developing at this time.

There were three forces that engendered a degree of pacification in this tumultuous society: the preaching of the friars, the justice provided in the royal courts, and the imprints upon society of the great aristocratic families, such as the House of Lancaster.

The friars—the Franciscans, the Dominicans, and the Carmelites—stimulated a spiritual awakening in late-fourteenth-century England. Among the manifestations of this awakening were religious processions and dramatic presentations of biblical scenes.

At one end of the spiritual scale, practices such as faith healing became ever more central to the religion of both the commoners and the nobility. At the other end of the spiritual scale, a flowering of mysticism and mystical writings occurred.

Religion became more privatized. Wealthy families and urban guilds established chantries, chapels that afforded a more secluded and intimate worship than was found in the traditional parish churches.

The system of royal justice set up in Henry II's time had given a central place to the meetings of the county courts twice a year, with itinerant royal justices presiding. The grand jury and, slowly, the jury of verdict became central to criminal procedure. Special panels of royal judges were sent out into the countryside to impanel juries to bring indictments against the organized gangs of bandits and demobilized soldiers, an effort that had some success.

Meanwhile the royal judges developed increasingly sophisticated procedures in property and inheritance cases and laid the foundation for the whole branch of common law concerned with liability (personal injury).

There were plenty of things wrong with the common law and the legal profession, including favoring the rich over the poor, and envelopment of the law courts in a mystique of obscurantism (as in American law today). But the judicial system, creaking along in its disorder, nevertheless contributed to the pacification of a violent society. The common law worked best at protecting the property of the gentry and nobility.

A third important factor in pacifying and stabilizing English society in the fourteenth century was the role played by the great aristocratic families, especially in areas relatively distant from the royal bureaucracy in London. These great families—the Lancastrians in northern England, the Percy and Neville families along the Scottish border—organized chains of social dependency that brought a degree of order and hierarchy into society, from the rural working class through the middle-class gentry.

Thousands of families were bound in loyalty and obedience to John of Gaunt and other great magnates. In this condition of passage from the medieval to the modern state, personal ties counted more than did the sinews of royal government in stabilizing a society that was experiencing the early impact of capitalism but lacked theory to identify the source of economic upheaval.

This was still a world in which lordship was very important. Who are you and your family? Tell me who your lord is, who dominates your county, and I can tell you what is your social status and personal credit.

Even merchants in the towns, in spite of their yearning for urban independence, fell into line, maintaining their association with aristocratic households, which were also their best customers.

Like the American billionaires of today, members of the high aristocracy exercised power and influence beyond their wealth and specific political connections. They exuded an aura of mastery. They set the fashion for high living. They transcended and at the same time stiffened the legal order disseminated by the royal judges and the religious hierarchy preached by friars and priests.

Men like Gaunt were not beyond criticism by the middle class in courts and parliaments or by protesting workers in the streets. But the aristocrats were beyond effective opposition and their word was law and faith. Gaunt and other great lords contributed mightily to the pacification and ordering of this increasingly inchoate and troubled society.

Only the king could strike down a great magnate and reduce his family to misery. And kings could do this only infrequently and in peril to themselves and their hold upon the throne. The classic case is that of Henry IV, Gaunt's son. Richard II harassed and mistreated the young Henry of Lancaster until the latter invaded England and removed his cousin from the throne.

CHAPTER FOUR

Women

I T WAS THE CUSTOM of Gaunt's father, King Edward III, and his Belgian queen, Philippa of Hainaut, to name their children after the places where they were born. Philippa gave birth to her fourth son, John, in 1340 in the industrial city of Ghent, where so much English wool was spun into woolen cloth. Ghent lay in Flanders, a couple of hundred miles from the small county of Hainaut. Both Flanders and Hainaut are incorporated into the modern state of Belgium. Ghent in England was pronounced "Gaunt," hence the name John of Gaunt.

As was usual with medieval kings, the marriage of Edward III to Philippa had some political significance. Ever since the time of Edward I (d. 1307), grandfather of Edward III, the English Crown had had an eye on Flanders, which was the market for England's main export product. Hainaut was no Flanders; it was a small and rural territory. But it bordered on Flanders as well as France, and Edward III by his marriage to Philippa gained a foothold in the Belgian world.

It was, however, a real love match. Edward III adored his vivacious, statuesque, and hardy wife. Together they produced seven children. Philippa inherited Hainaut from her father, and she made frequent visits to her homeland, even during one of her many pregnancies. That is how it happened that her son John was born in Ghent.

In the mid-fourteenth century a child was regarded as an infant until the age of seven and lived in a nursery surrounded by women. Only three years after leaving the nursery, John of Gaunt was in the military camp of his elder brother, the first son of Edward III and Philippa. This brother was a great knightly warrior, and he was the general when the English army won its two great victories at Crécy and Poitiers over the French king early in the Hundred Years' War.

The elder brother of John of Gaunt was Edward, Prince of Wales; he was the heir to the throne and was known as the Black Prince, from the color of his armor. He would never gain the throne, because his father reigned for four decades. Edward III was succeeded in 1377 by Richard II, the Black Prince's ten-year-old son by his much-adored wife, the beautiful Joan of Kent.

John of Gaunt grew up in the shadow of the Black Prince. He accompanied him on many campaigns in France and Spain. The ideals and behavior of his brother, John embraced as his own. The Black Prince's ideals and behavior pattern were those of the chivalric code—its belief in military prowess, treatment of other nobles with civility, and lifestyle of courtly love. The Black Prince was the most admired knight in Christendom.

Many in the nobility and gentry were honored to serve under Prince Edward. The Black Prince and his father founded the Order of the Garter, the most exclusive aristocratic club in Europe, modeled after King Arthur and the knights of the Round Table. The Order of the Garter exists today and bears an honorific aura still.

John of Gaunt grew up in the saddle, fighting alongside his brother in France and Spain until, when Gaunt was twenty-five, the Black Prince contracted malaria in Spain. The disease painfully enfeebled Prince Edward for the rest of his life. He had to withdraw from the battlefield, and John of Gaunt aimed to replace him as head of the English army.

The one time Gaunt was allowed to lead the English army in France, he demonstrated that he was no general. He marched his superb army around in a big circle for several months, never got the French to take up the challenge of battle, and accomplished nothing except to waste the resources that Parliament had provided through heavy taxation.

In his long lifetime, Gaunt fought in France, Spain, and the lowlands of Scotland. Only in the latter country did he gain a modicum of glory, if it was possible to gain glory by defeating the impoverished Scots.

The Black Prince set for his younger brother Gaunt examples beyond the chivalric code, which never had a place for generous treatment of the lower orders of society. After taking a French town through a long siege, the Prince of Wales killed all the male burgesses. He licensed "free companies" of knights to lay waste to the French countryside and slaughter the peasants. John of Gaunt too licensed companies of knights to devastate the western third of France.

Back in England the peasants were needed for their productivity. They were protected by the legal system. In France there was no restraint or respect. They could be slaughtered like rabbits and their property looted. The Church taught that the peasants had souls, but to the aristocracy and the wealthier gentry, the souls were dirty and of a lower grade. Absent the need for the peasants' labor and the protection afforded by the common law, peasants could be treated savagely.

This was the world in which Gaunt grew up and matured—from the exquisite clothing and cuisine and elegant manners of the Order of the Garter to slaughtered peasants in French fields. But even in England it was a world crumbling economically and with regard to public health. It was a world of poverty, terror, and death.

The economic and demographic expansion of Plantagenet England slowed and flattened out in the last two decades of the thirteenth century. All arable land was in use, and younger sons of the gentry and the peasants found real estate too expensive to purchase and thereupon establish households.

In the second decade of the fourteenth century there were crop failures and famine—for two summers the sun did not shine, being blotted out by great clouds of ash from volcanic eruptions in Indonesia. In 1346–1349, England was devastated by bubonic plague and anthrax, which carried off 40 percent of the population. Faith healing did not deliver protection from the Black Death.

An archaeological dig in Scotland has confirmed that the pestilence involved anthrax. An archaeological find in southern France confirms that bubonic plague was also at work in the Black Death. Anthrax was a cattle disease that migrated to humans. Bubonic plague was spread by fleas living on the backs of rats.

The royal family and the great lords offered no leadership to countervail the Black Death. Edward III, Philippa, and the Black Prince ran off to distant country estates until the pandemic had passed. But the Plantagenets could not entirely escape the shadow of the pandemic. Gaunt's young sister Joan, age twelve, was affianced to the heir to the throne of Castile. On her way through Gascony to reach Spain, Princess Joan died of the plague along with some of her entourage, including a Spanish minstrel, in the port town of Bordeaux, which was particularly susceptible to the spread of the Black Death. The mayor of Bordeaux, to stop the spread of disease, set fire to the port, and fire consumed an old Plantagenet castle on the waterfront. Joan's body was never recovered for burial.

But the biomedical disaster proved to be very fortunate for John of Gaunt. A new outbreak of the Black Death in 1361 killed his father-in-law, Henry Grosmont, Duke of Lancaster, leaving Gaunt to inherit Grosmont's property and eventually his title through Blanche, Gaunt's wife and Grosmont's daughter and heiress. This was the turning point in Gaunt's life.

Henry Grosmont, Duke of Lancaster, was the richest man in England next to the King and the Prince of Wales. He was literate and pious and was delighted to marry his youngest daughter, Blanche, to the son of Edward III and Philippa. He had another daughter, married to a Dutch lord. She would have shared Grosmont's estate with Blanche, but she died shortly after her father, leaving the whole vast estate, most of it in northern England, to Blanche and Gaunt.

⟲∞⟳

Blanche was fecund and lucky. Her son Henry Bolingbroke became King of England; her daughter Philippa, Queen of Portugal. Known, because of her name, as the White Duchess, Blanche was reputed to be a great beauty. The poet Geoffrey Chaucer, who wrote under Gaunt's patronage, has left this picture of her: "And good fair White she was called; that was my lady's very name. She was both fair and bright . . . She had right fair shoulders, and long body and arms, every limb plump and round but not over-large hands; full white and pink nails, round breasts, a straight flat back and hips of good breadth." According to Chaucer, Blanche's hair was "gold." "And what eyes my lady had! Gentle, good, glad, steadfast, simple, of good size, not too wide." She liked to sing and dance. (*The Book of the Good Duchess,* in *The Complete Poetical Works of Geoffrey Chaucer,* translated by J.S.P. Tatlock and P. MacKaye [New York: Macmillan, 1928]).

Is this the way Blanche really looked? Probably. It is certainly the way Gaunt wanted to remember her.

Chaucer's *Book of the Duchess* was an elegy on the recently deceased Blanche, written for the Duke. When he was dying early in 1399, Gaunt specified that he should be buried next to Blanche. His third wife was still alive. This was his former mistress Catherine Swynford. By this time Gaunt had forgotten about his second wife, Constance, the Castilian princess.

Blanche was everything chivalric culture prescribed in a woman. She was a faithful Guinevere, everything good that the Arthurian culture so heavily imbibed by the Knights of the Garter could conjure up about a woman. Gaunt loved Blanche dearly. She was the best thing in his life.

Blanche of Lancaster and Philippa of Hainaut. They stand out against an aristocratic horizon featuring strong and capable women. Joan of Kent, the wife of Edward the Black Prince, would be another outstanding woman of the late-fourteenth-century chivalric culture. Joan cared for the Black Prince through his many years of bad health.

This culture had achieved much in its impact upon the

great families, making their males more civil, literate, refined in taste, and admirable in deportment. These high nobles were unrestrained in their use of the arts of clothing, jewelry making, and cuisine, and in sponsoring domestic entertainment to amplify their status and exhibit fastidious tastes.

Fancy cloth was ordered from Flanders or Florence and turned into tunics, doublets, and gowns by master craftsmen, often aliens brought in for the purpose. Silks, imported by Italian merchants from East Asia, were greatly prized. Jewelry and aristocratic clothes were conjoined, since pearls and other precious stones were sewn right into the clothing.

What was special about cuisine were meat pies and elaborate desserts of custard or spun sugar. Barbecued meat was still the staple served at aristocratic tables, but the better chefs learned how to season the roasted or broiled meat with Oriental or Islamic spices. Pickled fish was also considered a delicacy.

Entertainment was minstrel poetry, recited and sung. Skilled performers were much in demand. They imbibed the Arthurian motifs, which included the celebration of the minds, hearts, and bodies of aristocratic and enormously wealthy women. In the romantic literature of the thirteenth century the usual theme was the perilous quest. The object of the quest could be spiritual—the Holy Grail, the cup from which Jesus drank at the Last Supper. It could be the body and mind of a golden-haired and highborn woman. Often it was both.

Chrétien de Troyes, a cleric writing at the court of Champagne in the late twelfth century, was the master of the literature of the perilous quest. Whether in pursuit of a kidnapped blond beauty or of the Holy Grail, the hero had to fight his way against a myriad of evil knights and monsters. The combat scenes and eroticism were much enjoyed by audiences in aristocratic households.

It is hard nowadays to give social credibility to chivalric culture, to see the lifestyle of the great families and their male exemplars like John of Gaunt as something historically important. However, their patronage of the arts of poetry, music, sculpture, and painting had a lasting impact on European civilization. Women found a prominent place in this refined and elaborate culture; this too would have enduring social impact. A subtle feminization of aristocratic life occurred.

Some handbooks prescribing conduct under the code of courtliness have survived. The woman's touch is prominent in these books on courtliness. "He who speaks badly of women is a boor for we are all born of women," says one such feminist clarion. "Be debonair . . . and see that you know how to speak *franceys*" is another piece of advice. Be moderate in all your behavior.

At table, "do not grab the tastiest morsels, or you will be reproached for being a rustic." When you belch, look up at the ceiling.

Cut back on sex and hot baths in summer (presumably to protect your health).

A well-brought-up great lord can not only ride and joust but also "play the harp, pipe, sing and dance." (All translations are by J. Gillingham.)

◦∞∞◦

The ancient Greeks saw little use for women except to produce children. The elite males of ancient Athenian society preferred homoerotic relationships. Their ideal beauty was the body of a ten-year-old boy.

The aristocrats of ancient Roma were more inclined toward heterosexuality than the Greeks, although they too greatly admired and sexually cultivated boys. There is a large body of heterosexual love poetry written in Latin from the ancient world.

The early medieval nobility derived from the Roman provincial aristocracy and the barbarian chieftains were decidedly heterosexual. But even noble women held a subservient place in early medieval society. They were defined in terms of their roles as mothers, mistresses, and nuns.

The shift toward a more egalitarian view of highborn women occurred in eleventh and twelfth-century Spain among the Muslims and Jews. The elite males in Iberian society still appreciated the bodies of boys. But they also expressed their erotic attachments to women of the upper class.

From Iberia, a new appreciation of feminine beauty and recognition of the free and equal status of highborn women migrated across the Pyrenees into Aquitaine in southwestern

France, and from there to the court of Champagne in northern France and then to the royal court in Paris.

The city of Narbonne, nestled in the foothills of the Pyrenees on the French side, was a bustling commercial city owned by its lord, Emmengard of Narbonne. Emmengard was addressed as "lord" even though she was a lady. At her court in the 1140s were troubadours writing and singing the new erotic poetry coming up from Muslim and Jewish Spain. Emmengard was a troubadour herself as well as a patroness of troubadours.

At least 10 percent, perhaps even 25 percent, of the population of Narbonne were Jews, most of them migrants from Spain. As the rabbis in Spain sought to impose on Iberian Jews a closer commitment to Talmudic learning and neotraditional observances, the highly literate Jewish mercantile class found in Narbonne under Emmengard's protection a freer world where an erotic culture could still be cultivated.

William X, Duke of Aquitaine, was a troubadour who passed down this liberal culture to his granddaughter Eleanor. One of Eleanor's daughters by her first marriage, to gloomy Louis VII of France, Marie, set up a great troubadour court in Champagne. By her second marriage, to Henry Plantagenet of England, Eleanor of Aquitaine gained the opportunity to introduce the erotic genre into English court circles.

It is significant that courtly romance always had about it a transgressive air, not only because of its intrinsic message of sexuality and adoration of women, but also because of the Jewish role in its early diffusion.

The fact that feudal property law allowed daughters to inherit estates in the absence of male heirs also contributed to an elevation in the status and wealth of aristocratic women in the Francophone world of the twelfth century.

The most important cause underlying the improvement in the status of aristocratic women was the existence of tough-minded daughters and wives in the great families in England as well as France.

Queen Mathilda, the mother of Henry II; Eleanor of Aquitaine, the queen of Henry II; Eleanor of Provence, the queen of Henry III and mother of Edward I; and Philippa of Hainaut, the queen of Edward III, showed the way to recognition of the independence of mind and high moral status of women in the great families. They served as models for women of the nobility. They had their own coteries of high-born ladies and favored knights and ever-ready priests who formed their courts.

The priests gave assurance and spiritual comfort to the highborn women and wrote treatises stressing their equal status with males in their families and communities. Courtly love—heterosexual—was given ambivalent clerical approval.

Dress was erotically provocative. The high line of aristocratic women's dresses brought attention to their breasts. Men showed off their legs in court dress, and their short doublets focused attention on the male sex organ.

Paintings and sculptures highlighted the shape of both men's and women's bodies. The portrayal of the Virgin as Madonna was often sexually suggestive. In Paris and Florence painters and sculptors were showing a new appreciation for the contours of the human body, especially that of the female.

Above all, in aristocratic courts the centrality of the theme of heterosexual love in poetry recited daily, often to music, gave legitimacy to intimate relations between the sexes. It was something, this emphasis on heterosexual love, including promiscuity and adultery, that John of Gaunt had drummed into his ears several evenings a week, and he behaved accordingly. The poets and musicians adored highborn women and advocated their prominent and autonomous place in society.

John of Gaunt's own behavior showed his appreciation of such women and his dependence on them. His life was marked by the three women he married, each so distinct from the others. He fathered nine children by them.

Blanche of Lancaster represented for Gaunt everything good in his life. He gave her his unstinting admiration and love. She was the dream woman. She was the kind of white shining feminine figure that appeared often in poetry of the era. She was remembered by Gaunt through a halo of gold. That she was the richest heiress in England who brought Gaunt the foundation of his enormous wealth and his title of Duke of Lancaster only made Blanche the more to be revered, and remembered as a kind of saint. Gaunt buried Blanche in an elaborate tomb in London and shared the tomb with her when he died.

Gaunt's second wife, Constance, the legitimate but unlucky heiress to the throne of Castile, was treated very differently by Gaunt than Blanche was. Eventually Constance was shunted off and forgotten. Even though Gaunt was inclined to treat women of the aristocracy and gentry with consideration and respect, he mistreated Constance.

Their marriage in 1369 was a diplomatic one, made so that Gaunt could claim the throne of Castile through Constance. They did, however, cohabit long enough to produce one child, a daughter named Catherine. Constance's claim to the Castilian throne was successfully contested by her cousins Henry of Trástamara and Juan I from the illegitimate line of the Castilian dynasty, which had the support of the nobility and the towns.

Under the terms of a deal that Gaunt made with the King of Castile in 1387, Gaunt and Constance forfeited their claim to the Castilian throne for a great sum of money, and their daughter married the heir to that throne. From this marriage came a line of Castilian monarchs who were descended from Gaunt.

Constance was totally deferential to her husband and did not complain of her loss of her legitimate claim to the Castilian throne. There was, however, nothing left of love between John of Gaunt and Constance. After their return to England, he parked her on a distant Lancastrian estate until her death a few years later.

Constance was buried in the city of Leicester, probably on the grounds of a nunnery. Hers had not been a happy life. The daughter and heiress of Pedro the Cruel and also Duchess of Lancaster by her marriage to John of Gaunt, she died alone and in obscurity. In effect, Gaunt betrayed her and then abandoned her. She was not a member of the Anglo-French elite. She was a poor little rich girl from Spain.

Perhaps one reason Gaunt treated Constance so differently than he had treated Blanche can be found in another attachment. For many years Gaunt had maintained a relationship with Catherine Swynford, who came from the Belgian gentry and had immigrated to England with her father, one of the entourage of Queen Philippa of Hainaut, and her sister, who became Geoffrey Chaucer's wife. The sister, also named Philippa, perhaps also briefly was another in Gaunt's string of mistresses.

This Belgian woman, born Catherine de Roet, was Gaunt's long-standing mistress and, after Blanche, the great love of his life. At the time she met Gaunt, Catherine was married to a member of the upper gentry named Sir Hugh Swynford. After she had a child by Swynford, she became involved with Gaunt, and her marriage to Swynford became nominal and asexual. Hugh Swynford died on a military campaign in France. Gaunt continued his relationship with Catherine and had four children by her. He placed Catherine in the position of governess to Blanche's two daughters and she raised them after Blanche died.

Five years before his death, Gaunt married Catherine, to the shock of aristocratic Europe, and he took great pains to have his family by her legitimated. Their offspring were given the name Beaufort. One of them, Henry Beaufort, received a Latinate education and became a bishop and later a cardinal. He was an important politician in the next generation at the court of his nephew Henry V.

A daughter of Catherine and Gaunt named Margaret Beaufort married Edmund Tudor, the son of Henry V's widow and her Master of the Horse, a young Welshman by the name of Owen Tudor. Margaret and Edmund's son was Henry, Earl of Richmond. A Lancastrian, he would overthrow the Yorkist king Richard III, marry Elizabeth of York, and rule as Henry VII. Thus the Wars of the Roses ended and the Tudor dynasty was born.

Gaunt showered gifts on Catherine Swynford—expensive jewelry, fine cloth for gowns. He also gave her more mundane gifts, such as barrels of red wine from Bordeaux and wood for her fireplaces. He deeded Lancastrian manorial properties to her so that she would always have a steady income.

Catherine was a vivacious and shrewd woman who blended in easily at the royal court. She got along with Alice Perrers, old Edward III's mistress.

The relationship between Gaunt and Catherine was founded neither on aristocratic courtliness nor on diplomacy

Two knights jousting.

John of Gaunt.

Tomb of Edward the
Black Prince.
ANGELO HORNAK

The Black Prince.
THE BRITISH LIBRARY

The Battle of Crécy.

The Battle of Poitiers, showing French crossbowmen and English longbow archers.

King Edward III in robes of the Order of the Garter.

Geoffrey Chaucer.

The marriage of Philippa, daughter of John of Gaunt, and João I of Portugal.

Genealogy of Philippa,
daughter of John of Gaunt.

John of Gaunt entertained by João I of Portugal.

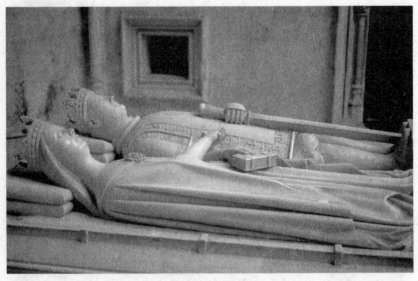

The tomb of King João I of Portugal and Philippa, daughter of John of Gaunt.

The coronation of King Richard II, nephew of John of Gaunt.

Richard II dines with John of Gaunt and other dukes.

Richard II enters the Tower of London, dispatched there by Henry Bolingbroke, son of John of Gaunt.

The fall of a homosexual king: the funeral of Richard II.

and politics. It arose from carnal passion that was surprisingly long-lived. Gaunt found Catherine physically attractive, clever, and accommodating. He came to love his children by her, and this, coupled with his advancing age and the fact that there were no more thrones to yearn for, made it possible for him to flout custom and public opinion and marry her.

There are many things we can say about Gaunt. Among them is that he was a man who loved women and was obviously loved in return.

CᴙᴙᴙƆ

Five hundred pages of Gaunt's business letters have survived, but not one personal letter. There is no evidence from late medieval England that aristocrats wrote personal letters at that time. From mid-fifteenth-century England there have survived many letters from the Paston family, upper-level gentry who held extensive lands in East Anglia. One of the Paston letters is from a prominent member of the family, away on business, to his wife, expressing his sexual longing for her. But from an aristocrat there is no comparable personal letter.

If John of Gaunt *had* written to his mistress Catherine Swynford, it might have been along these lines:

My beloved Cate: I hope you received the wood from my estates, the two barrels of Bordeaux claret, and the pearl necklace from Egypt that I sent you. It is now four years since I first saw you in the Nursery taking care of my two daughters. I was immediately struck by your beauty and the fine figure of a woman you represented. I admired your breasts in particular. Constance, the Spanish wife smelling of garlic and olive oil, was still alive. But the first time I saw you, I knew I had found the woman to replace my late lamented Blanche. The first time I slept with you I knew you would be the great love of my later years. Now that you are pregnant with our child, our love will be long-enduring. Take good care of yourself. Lancaster.

Gaunt was a passionate man, and women meant a great deal to him. By the time he married Catherine Swynford his military career had ended, at the age of fifty-five. Contrary to rumor at the time, he did not want to supplant his nephew Richard II as King of England. Gaunt undoubtedly would have liked to be king, but there is no indication that he was willing to usurp the throne from his nephew. On the contrary, Gaunt tried to prop up Richard II.

Therefore the two other things in life that meant the most to him—being a great military leader and taking the kingship—were cut off for Gaunt by 1396. What was left was to fulfill his personal happiness with the woman he loved. Courtiers might sneer at the high aristocrat who married his commoner mistress. Members of royal families elsewhere in Europe might be scandalized. Gaunt did not care. Getting on in years, he chose the route of personal happiness. Only someone of his wealth, status, and bloodline among the aristocracy could do that.

Gaunt was one of those men who get along better with women than with men. This condition is not uncommon today but was rare in the Middle Ages, given the patriarchal nature of society.

Gaunt had thousands of male followers and colleagues. But he lacked a close male friend other than his brother Edward the Black Prince, who died in 1376. Gaunt had been respectful of, but distant toward, his father, Edward III. He had been on closer terms with his mother, Philippa of Hainaut. He was friendly with Joan of Kent, the Black Prince's widow. He seems to have had no problem with Alice Perrers, old Edward III's mistress, and he protected her from her middle-class enemies in Parliament.

Above all, there were his first wife, Blanche of Lancaster, and his long-standing mistress and third wife, Catherine Swynford. Aside from the Black Prince, they were his closest friends.

What Gaunt most enjoyed, apart from being in a military camp in France or Spain, was a two-week Christmas holiday at one of his country residences, to which he would invite hundreds of people, including many women. After luxurious dining, he would listen again to the stories of Arthur, Guinevere, and Lancelot. He would relish some new love story a poet had dreamed up.

After song and story, Gaunt would dance with some of the assembled ladies, showing off his fine legs and well-proportioned body. Essentially, the Christmas feast was a women's world, and Gaunt relished it. In aristocratic courts women ruled or at least shared rule with civilized and courteous male aristocrats like Gaunt.

One can apply to Gaunt a remark in *The Romance of the Horn* about an elegant and well-dressed man at table in an aristocratic household: "No lady seeing him was not deeply affected and troubled by the pangs of love . . . did not want to hold him softly to her under an ermine coverlet." (Translated by J. Weiss and J. Gillingham.)

In the 1950s Norbert Elias published a famous work of historical sociology in which he attributed to French courts of the early modern era the coming of *civilitas,* compared to alleged medieval wildness in behavior. We know now that Elias's dichotomy was wrong. Gaunt was already a civilized person, amenable to feminine ideals of aristocratic behavior.

❧

A monk at St. Alban's Abbey, writing shortly after Gaunt died, said that Gaunt's greatest defect was lechery. There was a widespread conviction in clerical circles that lechery and promiscuity were rife in high social circles. A papal inquisitor writing at the end of the fifteenth century observed: "The world is full of adultery and fornication especially in the palaces of princes and wealthy men." He wrote that it was "the time of women" and "mad love." (Translated by J. Delumeau and E. Nicolson in *Sin and Fear* [New York: St. Martin's Press, 1991]).

Perhaps 25 percent of the manuals for clerical confessors in the late Middle Ages is taken up with counseling people, especially males, with regard to their guilty avowals of lust and lechery. As might be expected, the advice given in confessors' manuals runs the gamut from the extremely rigorous—sexual relations between men and women are allowed only for purposes of procreation, and pleasure during intercourse is balefully sinful—to somewhat more liberal opinions. A thirteenth-century English Franciscan moralist, Richard Middleton, defends "moderate pleasure." Jean Gerson, the leading theologian at the University of Paris in the second decade of the fifteenth century, thought that seeking pleasure within marriage was a venial (pardonable) sin.

There has been a trend in recent writing on late medieval sexuality to take very seriously the admonitions of the antisexual rigorists against carnal love within marriage and their absolute horror at fornication outside of marriage. These strictures, however, do not seem to have limited the actual indulgence in sexual relations between men and women.

Sexuality was a normal part of life, along with eating and defecation. Everyone knew that the priests were trained to hear or even elicit accounts of sexual misbehavior in confession. That did not restrict everyday behavior. Intercourse was engaged in freely as it is today, even though contraception of any kind was practiced only by a very small minority of the population.

John of Gaunt was a strong case in point. He seems to have fully satisfied himself sexually, if not with wives then with mistresses. There were things that frustrated him on the battlefield, in politics, or in trying to control rebellious peasants, but all evidence indicates that he lived a quite free and healthy sexual life. Sexual repression was not his problem. Perhaps Gaunt varied from the norm only in being very generous to his bastard children, whereas other male aristocrats often neglected theirs.

It is necessary to stress Gaunt's free sexual behavior not only to round out our picture of the man, but to countervail recent views of the later Middle Ages as a dark time of sexual repression. Citing medieval confessors' manuals on sexual relations proves nothing. You could find similar rigorous proscription of sex and incitement of guilt about it in confessors' manuals today. The moral regimen priests were urged to impose upon the laity was no more significant in Gaunt's time than today.

CHAPTER FIVE

WARRIORS

J OHN OF GAUNT GREW UP in a nursery along with two sisters and two brothers in England under the watchful eye of his mother, Philippa. When he was an infant, Gaunt had his own cradle-rocker. The nursery was serviced by a half-dozen nurses and two governesses.

From the age of five to the age of ten, Gaunt was educated in written French, and some Latin, and in English. To be able to speak and write fluent French was the chief aim of his education. There were numerous textbooks from which to learn French and Latin. Gaunt probably learned English orally and, if he wanted to write a note in English, sounded out the words as he had heard them. There was no standard English until the late fifteenth century.

By the age of eight, Gaunt, with the help of a tutor, was reading extracts from French romances. By age ten he could read any French romance and the simpler kinds of Latin writings.

Probably from the age of five, Gaunt was trained to ride; he was always an exceptional horseman and he later took an interest in breeding horses, cross-breeding French with Arabic strains. By age ten Gaunt was well-instructed in the essentials of knightly warfare both on horseback and in hand-to-hand fighting, and by age fourteen he would be knighted as the Earl of Richmond.

But at age ten Gaunt was deemed ready to experience warfare personally. While he was crossing the English Channel to the camp of Edward the Black Prince, the small fleet his ship was in was intercepted by a Spanish squadron and he found himself in the midst of hand-to-hand fighting between the English and Spanish crews. Once Gaunt got to the Black Prince's camp he was ready for advanced training in knightly warfare.

He was participating in battles by age thirteen and at age fifteen was fighting alongside his father, Edward III, on the Scottish frontier. When at the age of nineteen he married Blanche, heiress to the great Duchy of Lancaster, Gaunt was ready to take a leading role in war and peace.

As he was growing up, John, like his brothers, would have read several volumes, mostly in French, some in simple Latin, that made up the *Mirror of Princes* literature popular at the time. Since these short tomes were written by university scholars educated in the Aristotelian tradition, the principles the *Mirror of Princes* inculcated was drawn heavily from Aristotle's *Ethics* and *Politics*.

The *Mirror* urged the practice of the Golden Mean, moderate day-to-day behavior. In politics it favored a balanced constitution, leaning markedly toward an aristocratic elite that showed responsibility to the needs and feelings of the people and practiced a kind of enlightened despotism. Gaunt would also have read an ecclesiastical treatise or two on the sacredness of kingship and how the royal balm of coronation elevated the king's political body above that of anyone else. Since Gaunt was not the heir to the throne, but only a backup, he probably was not very interested in the kingship tracts, although throughout his life he respected the authority of the Crown.

This reading did increase his respect for his brother Edward the Black Prince, who as Prince of Wales was the heir to the throne. It was not political theory but the Black Prince's deeds on the battlefield that especially earned Gaunt's devotion.

Gaunt's childhood and education were standard for a prince of his day. He was precocious in being introduced to battlefield and military camp conditions in his tenth year.

◦◦◦

John of Gaunt and his elder brother Edward the Black Prince loved armed combat during war. Tournaments were very enjoyable, but it was actual declared war against France and the clash of armored cavalry on the battlefield that enthralled them. When Edward III declared a truce with the King of

France to be nullified and sent summons to war to the nobility and gentry, this was the moment that Gaunt and the Black Prince had been anticipating. Now they would prepare themselves and summon their huge retinues to go to France.

The English already used infantry with longbows in their armies. They had learned this manner of fighting from the Welsh, and indeed they relied heavily on Welsh soldiers. But this tactical approach was not what really excited the Black Prince and Gaunt. The part of the English army that interested them and in which they participated was the armored cavalry. Armor and horses, banners and trumpets, these were accouterments of wars worth fighting.

Tell Gaunt and his elder brother that military future might lie with the infantry, whose arrows could at close range sometimes penetrate armor or at least bring down a knight's horse, and they would not have been enthusiastic. Their idea of warfare was no different from that of the French nobility, who were sometimes their kin.

They relished putting on heavy plate armor and fancy helmets with visors protecting their faces. They were delighted by their huge horses, akin to the Clydesdales we see pulling yesteryear's brewery wagons. They held their long lances in front of them, alongside and protruding beyond their horses' heads, and charged their opponents, trying to unseat the enemy knights.

Just as much as fighting on horseback, the Black Prince and Gaunt enjoyed hand-to-hand battle on foot with their long, heavy swords—the clash of steel upon steel. This was the culmination of half a millennium of development in warfare. This was chivalry in a material sense.

It took thousands of hours of training and practice in tournaments and a very powerful physique to do this kind of fighting successfully. The battles began with companies of knights charging against each other's lines, but it was the individual challenges on horse and foot that provided the greatest pleasure on the battlefield.

The French nobility discovered, after tremendous defeats in two battles early in the Hundred Years' War, that they lacked some quality that would allow them to contend as equals against the Black Prince and Gaunt. After those defeats, with hundreds of knights and some great lords, including a king of France, held for ransom, the French avoided pitched battles and resorted to skirmishes, guerrilla warfare, walled towers, and protracted defenses against sieges.

There was also the camaraderie of the campaign to delight the brothers. Each lord had his tent where he could serve as host to his friends. The smell of roasting meat filled the air. The tapping of barrels of red wine and beer led to raucous talk and singing. Minstrels sang of the epic deeds of great warriors from the time of Charlemagne on. And then there were the whores, the camp followers.

Even if the campaign did not go well as the French refused battle, as the countryside was already picked clean of supplies, as rain pelted down on the English army, the Black

Prince and Gaunt and their coterie of cousins and friends still had the warmth of each other's presence. This is what they had been bred and trained for. This was the military life that justified their aristocratic privileges and great estates.

That they were decimating the French countryside, stripping it of grain and domestic animals, did not bother them. The priests and friars who accompanied the army did not raise this uncomfortable point. War and its ravages upon the peasantry was an acceptable force of nature. Only the woeful accounts of the monastic chroniclers remind us of the pitiable downside of the Hundred Years' War.

Women of the aristocracy were not entirely excluded from military campaigns. Sometimes wives of the great lords would visit an encampment briefly. But going to war was a male preoccupation. In royal and aristocratic courts, women's presence was a strong one. Warfare was a man's world. The great lords may have written letters to their wives back in England, but here in the encampments and on the battle-field, it was horses that were more in the forefront of every-day concern than women.

The wives and families of the lords and knights came within urgent reference when warriors faced imminent death, or were seriously wounded, or captured on the battle-field and held for ransom. The warriors were concerned that their wives and children would be taken care of appropriately and, if the warriors died, would come into their suitable inheritances.

For a widow this inheritance normally meant a dower, one-third of the income of the husband's estate until the dowager died. However, many landed properties were held jointly by lord and lady, and in such cases the widow recovered the property itself at her husband's death, not just the income. Inheritance came by primogeniture—inheritance by sons, the eldest getting most of the property and the aristocratic title. Failing male heirs, daughters could inherit. That is how John of Gaunt came into the Duchy of Lancaster.

Lawyers worked complex inheritance settlements before the lords and knights went to fight on the Continent. The eldest male heir got by law at least 90 percent of his deceased father's estate. The main heir's estates were "entailed." He was to have the income for life, but he could not sell off the inherited lands. There were small portions for younger sons and provision for dowries for daughters.

The Black Prince and Gaunt and the other great lords were mindful of what would happen to their families in the event of their deaths overseas in battle. As much as they enjoyed war and military encampments, they were not inclined to be reckless or improvident.

The English wars in France as well as frequent fighting along the frontier with Scotland were paid for mainly by taxes granted by Parliament, supplemented by aristocrats drawing upon their own resources. Unless there was a great victory that resulted in booty, loot, and highborn captives held for ransom, English aristocrats like the Black Prince and Gaunt did not actually make money out of warfare. They probably ran somewhere near 20 percent in the red, or so we are told by Gaunt's records and those of the English Exchequer.

The gentry and burgesses represented in Parliament would not, however, let the warrior aristocracy forget that the greater part of the cost of war was paid out of grants of Parliament-approved taxes that fell heaviest on the gentry and merchant class.

Failure of an expedition to achieve promised results was likely to have political repercussions. The Black Prince's military ventures were never criticized. Gaunt, less successful than his brother as a general, was occasionally reprimanded in Parliament for wasting national resources.

Their families having been insured by lawyers' instruments against the consequences of their mortality, Gaunt and the great lords, as well as fighting gentry who were their retainers, could go off to war with familial anxiety eased.

⟨⟩⟩

War and especially famous victories produce important memories or myths about battles. Historians are still debating the main cause of the British victory at El Alamein in North Africa in 1942, the first Allied victory in the war against Hitler. Was it due to the brilliant tactical skill of the British commander, General Bernard Montgomery? Was it due to the superiority in firepower that Montgomery enjoyed? Was it due to the temporary absence on sick leave in Germany of the German commander, the Desert Fox whom the Allies feared, General Erwin Rommel? Some writers even attribute the victory at El Alamein to the strategic planning of General Claude Auchinleck, Montgomery's predecessor and head of the British army in North Africa.

For Gaunt it was what the Black Prince accomplished at Crécy in 1346 and Poitiers in 1356 that was the ultimate in aristocratic warfare. The main narrative account of the greatest victory of the English army in the Hundred Years' War, under Edward III and the Black Prince, at the Battle of Crécy, is provided by Jean Froissart. Froissart was a French-speaking Belgian, from the lower ranks of the nobility, who accompanied Philippa of Hainaut to England and remained as court historian for three decades, eventually turning out twenty volumes. Here is his classic account of why the English won at Crécy:

> The English, who were drawn up in three divisions, and seated on the ground, on seeing their enemies advance, rose undauntedly up, and fell into their ranks. That of the prince was the first to do so, whose archers were formed in the manner of a portcullis or harp, and the men-at-arms in the rear. The earls of Northampton and Arundel, who commanded the second division, had posted themselves in good order on his wing, to assist and succor the prince, if necessary.

You must know, that these kings, earls, barons and lords of France, did not advance in any regular order, but one after the other, or any way most pleasing to themselves. But as soon as the king of France came in sight of the English, his blood began to boil, and cried out to his marshals, "Order the Genoese forward, and begin the battle, in the name of God and St. Denis." There were about fifteen thousand Genoese crossbow-men; but they were quite fatigued, having marched on foot that day six leagues, completely armed, and with their crossbows. They told the constable, they were not in a fit condition to do great things that day in battle. The earl of Alençon, hearing this, said, "This is what one gets by employing such scoundrels, who fall off when there is any need for them." During this time a heavy rain fell, accompanied by thunder and a very ter-rible eclipse of the sun; and before this rain a great flight of crows hovered in the air over all those battal-ions making a loud noise. Shortly afterwards it cleared up, and the sun shone very bright; the Frenchmen had it in their faces, and the English in their backs. When the Genoese were somewhat in order, and approached the English, they set up a loud shout, in order to frighten them; but they remained quite still, and did not seem to attend to it. They set up a second shout, and advanced a little forward; but the English never moved.

The first division, seeing the danger they were in, sent a knight in great haste to the king of England, who was posted upon an eminence, near a windmill. On the knight's arrival, he said, "Sir, the earl of Warwick, the lord Stafford, the lord Reginald Cobham, and the others who are about your son, are vigorously attacked by the French; and they entreat that you would come to their assistance with your battalion, for, if their numbers should increase, they fear he will have too much to do." The king replied, "Is my son dead, unhorsed, or so badly wounded that he cannot support himself?" "Nothing of the sort, thank God," rejoined the knight; "but he is in so hot an engagement that he has great need of your help." The king answered, "Now, sir Thomas, return back to those that sent you, and tell them from me, not to send again for me this day, or expect that I shall come, let what will happen, as long as my son has life; and say, that I command them to let the boy win his spurs; for I am determined, if it please God, that all the glory and honour of this day shall be given to him, and to those into whose care I have intrusted him." The knight returned to his lords, and related the king's answer, which mightily encouraged them, and made them repent they had ever sent such a message . . .

The earl of Blois, nephew to the king of France, and the duke of Lorraine, his brother-in-law, with their troops, made a gallant defense; but they were surrounded by a troop of English and Welsh, and slain in spite of their prowess. The earl of St. Pol and the earl of Auxerre were also killed, as well as many others. Later after vespers, the king of France had not more about him than sixty men, every one included. Sir John of Hainault, who was of the number had once remounted the king, for his horse had been killed under him by an arrow, he said to the king, "Sir, retreat whilst you have an opportunity, and do not expose yourself so simply; if you have lost this battle, another time you will be the conqueror." After he had said this, he took the bridle of the king's horse, and led him off by force; for he had before entreated of him to retire. The king rode on until he came to the castle of la Broyes, where he found the gates shut, for it was very dark. The king ordered the governor of it to be summoned: he came upon the battlements, and asked who it was that called at such an hour? The king answered, "Open, open, governor, it is the fortune of France." The governor, hearing the king's voice, immediately descended, opened the gate, and let down the bridge. The king and his company entered the castle; but he had only with him five barons, sir John of Hainault, the lord Charles of Montmorency, the lord of Beaujeu, the lord of Aubigny, and the lord of Montfort. The king would not bury himself in such a place as that, but having taken some refreshments, set out again with his attendants about midnight, and rode on, under the direction of guides who were well acquainted with the country, until about daybreak, he came to Amiens, where he halted. This Saturday the English never quitted their ranks in pursuit of anyone, but remained on the field, guarding their position, and defending themselves against all who attacked them. The battle was ended at the hour of vespers.

Thus Froissart tells us—in an account absorbed by generations of British schoolchildren—that the English won the great victory at Crécy because they were much better organized and less hotheaded than the French; that Edward III was cool and tactically shrewd; that the French king was personally brave but anguished and confused; that the Genoese bowmen hired by the French were unprepared for battle.

Is Froissart's account true? We have no way of knowing, since it is the only detailed account of the battle. We do know that he was not an eyewitness to the battle and that he wrote his account at least a decade after it took place. His story is replete with literary stereotypes and tropes flattering to the English and their leaders. Maybe Froissart got his account from courtiers who were present, or who got their account from lords who were actually there. Maybe.

Interestingly, contemporary accounts of the great victory of Henry V, John of Gaunt's grandson, over the French at Agincourt in 1415 tell very much the same story: English organized and cool; French disorganized and hotheaded.

This account made its way into Shakespeare's *Henry V* and into Laurence Olivier's great 1944 film (made in Ireland and using half the Irish army).

Were the English perpetually so shrewd and the French perpetually so stupid? We don't know. When Kenneth Branagh came to do his untraditional version of *Henry V* in 1989, he played down the battle, using as soldiers what appear to be six drinkers he picked up in a pub. But Olivier had to do it gloriously in 1944 because the war-weary Brits needed a psychological lift. Shakespeare too had to hype Agincourt, because the English army of his day was so puny that Queen Elizabeth I was afraid to fight on the Continent. Military history is elusive, giving opportunity to mythmakers like Jean Froissart.

༄

For Gaunt, warfare always meant his association with his elder brother. It was Edward the Black Prince who had accepted him at his military camp when Gaunt was ten years old. He had trained Gaunt personally in the difficult arts of war. Gaunt emulated the Black Prince and they enjoyed battlefield victories together. For Gaunt, being a warrior, fighting as a mounted knight in full armor, was an expression of fraternal love and obsessive admiration for his brother.

When Prince Edward contracted malaria in Spain and had to retire to his home in England for a long and terminal illness under the care of his wife, Joan of Kent, how lonely it was for Gaunt to continue military expeditions without the Black Prince at his side. How Gaunt missed the strategy, charismatic leadership, and constant high spirits that the Black Prince provided. Some great life force went out of Plantagenet war making.

The burdens of leadership and strategy remained for Gaunt, but the emotional, frenetic side of warfare, the great game of knighthood, had diminished immeasurably with the withdrawal of the Black Prince into his long decrepitude.

Now the logistical and bureaucratic side of war, the raising of money, the recruitment of knights and men-at-arms (infantry), the marshaling of ships, the reading of coastal maps to decide where to land in France and what route then to follow, and the feeding and paying of army regiments, all these cares now fell principally on Gaunt's shoulders, and he keenly felt these cares.

The romance of war diminished for Gaunt and the business side of military life became more pressing. Because he was a man who shouldered his royal responsibilities and obligations willingly, he did what was required of him, but war was never exhilarating again.

There were some three hundred officials who did Gaunt's business, seeing to it that, from a variety of sources, the Duke would have the resources for campaigns in France and Spain and skirmishes along the Scottish march (border). As much or more income was needed to sustain the Duke's lifestyle.

At one point Gaunt wrote to his treasurer and asked for

some pocket money. The official sent him twenty-three pounds sterling, about $300,000 in today's money. Gaunt was a man who lived in the context of cash flow.

Gaunt's net income from his estates was around seven thousand pounds sterling per year. But in any given year the income from his estates could be at least matched by income from other sources, such as his share of the proceeds of parliamentary taxation to pay for military expeditions.

Seven thousand pounds in the the late fourteenth century is equal to at least a half-billion American dollars a year today. Therefore, in many years of his mature lifetime, Gaunt received an income that amounted to at least a billion dollars.

The capital value of his estates, houses, and movable property (jewels, artwork) would come to $100 billion in our money. The laws of property allowed him to borrow against his estates, but not to sell off any significant proportion of them.

His wartime expenditures stretched even Gaunt's enormous resources. He did not have the liquid assets to outfit an appropriate army in his Spanish campaign. (Hollywood films give no idea of the massive costs of outfitting, transporting, and maintaining a military force in late medieval wars.)

A function of the ducal officials was to make sure that every scrap of military service owed the Duke by gentry and knights was actually provided. Then all officials had to make sure that when the Duke granted money, pensions, land, wood, or live deer to someone, the disbursement was actually made. They had to manage this using only pens writing on pieces of parchment. They employed dozens of messengers, who fanned out over the countryside on horseback. There was no other means of long-distance communication.

There were four kinds of ducal officials. First there was the approximately ten-person council of wealthy and experienced nobility and gentry, headed by a chancellor, usually a bishop on extended leave from his diocese. There was an administrative office that the chancellor supervised, comprising two dozen clerks and a half-dozen lawyers.

Then there were the stewards, who managed the Duke's estates. Next were the receivers, treasury officials charged with collecting rents, taxes, and other moneys owed the Duke; making disbursements authorized by the Duke or a member of his council; and keeping careful financial records. Finally there were "feodars," who were responsible for making sure that the Duke got the military service owed him under one kind of feudal contract or another. Obviously the feodars were especially busy in time of war.

◎⁓◎

All these matters were set down in copies of outgoing letters and documents in the Duke's Register. The letters and documents were sent out by the Duke or by his chancellor or another member of his council. Chivalry was sustained by bureaucracy.

Of course, the King's government and that of the great

aristocrats ran on similar lines. Thus was an element of reason and a high degree of literacy introduced into warrior society.

Like the archives of an American billionaire capitalist of today, the Register of John of Gaunt includes hundreds of documents of a strictly business nature. Here is a typical indenture or contract for military service between the Duke and a member of the gentry:

> Indenture between John, Duke of Lancaster, and Sir Thomas de Erpyngham. Sir Thomas to serve the duke for life in peace and war, and to go with him to war wherever he wishes, with an esquire, etc., suitably arrayed for war; to receive in time of peace, for himself and his esquire, £20 a year from the manor of Gimingham in Norfolk, and to have wages and food at court whenever sent by command of the duke. In time of war to receive for himself and his esquire 50 marks a year and to have wages or food as other bachelors [knights] of his rank. For horses lost in the duke's service, for the beginning of his year of war, for prisoners of war and other booty taken by himself or his men, and for the freight of himself and his men and horses, the duke to do for him as for other bachelors of his rank.
>
> *Translated by E. C. Lodge*

For the indenture to be valid, Sir Thomas would have had to affix his seal to a copy of the document and return the piece of parchment to the Duke's chancellor.

Like all great English aristocrats (including some today), Gaunt controlled the property of thousands of parish churches and thereby also controlled the right of appointment of the priests to the churches, with nominal approval of a bishop. Similarly, Gaunt controlled the prebends, or endowments, that supported cathedral clergy. Here is a typical example:

> Presentation to John, bishop of Lincoln, of Master Thomas Brightwell, doctor in theology, of the diocese of Salisbury, for admission to a prebend in the collegiate church of St. Mary, Leicester, vacant by the death of Robert Broghton.
>
> *Translated by E. C. Lodge*

Even in the midst of war, some of the letters in the Duke's Register deal with family matters. The two favorite women of his later years, his daughter Philippa and his mistress Catherine Swynford, are to be well taken care of:

> Order to Adam Pope, clerk, receiver in the county of Norfolk, to pay to William Oke, clerk of the duke's great wardrobe, £50 sterling assigned for the wardrobe and chamber [treasury] of the duke's daughter Philippa of Lancaster, for Michaelmas last, receiving letters of acquitance under his seal; also to pay to lady Katerine de Swynneford £100 a year in equal portions at Easter

and Michaelmas for the expenses of the chamber and wardrobe of the duke's daughter, receiving letters of acquittance under her seal.

Register, translated by E. C. Lodge

Catherine was Philippa's governess at the time.

Favorite churchmen also had to be rewarded. A favorite gift of the Duke to a religious house or order was wood from his chase (hunting ground). Thereby a group of Franciscan friars, for example, received cut-up wood from six oak trees and had a warm winter.

The Archbishop of Canterbury, according to Gaunt's Register, received a more generous gift: a dozen "live does" from the Duke's chase.

What is amazing about the Duke's Register is the careful recording of everything done in his name by his administrators. In a given year hundreds of pages of parchment were used up by his chancery. In fact, one of the items in the Register refers to an urgent requisition of additional ink and parchment.

The Duke lived an itinerant life, and his needs and those of his household had to be taken care of under mobile conditions. When a parliament was held in Northampton instead of London, about $200,000 was set aside for "purchases and purveyances [food] . . . for the Duke's sojourn during the coming parliament to be held there." A parliament lasted about three weeks; the letter quoted gives an idea

of Gaunt's lifestyle and the size of his itinerant household—
about a hundred people.

Spiritual needs of the Duke had also to be reckoned with
when he moved about. In 1381, as the Duke was heading for
an extended stay at one of his castles, his private chapel had
to come with him.

> Order to John de Grantham, dean of the duke's chapel,
> and William Dyer, clerk of the same, to pack up as well
> as possible all jewels, vestments and ornaments of the
> said chapel, ready to be carried to the castle of Ponte-
> fract, as the duke, with the advice and assent of his
> council, has ordered his household to be there for a cer-
> tain time, and to come there themselves with all the
> clerks and ministers of the chapel. Order for the car-
> riage of the aforesaid goods has been sent to William
> Chesuldene, receiver of Leicester.
>
> *Register, translated by E. C. Lodge*

There are many requisitions in the Duke's Register for
building houses on his estates, repairing old ones, and repairing roads and bridges. When Gaunt moved, he wanted everything to be in good shape on the estate he visited and the
roads and bridges to offer easy and rapid access. His castles
were to be well guarded by soldiers and archers.

Gaunt's most important business was ultimately on the
battlefield. These warrior moments were his shining ones, in
his view.

To make this battlefield combat maximally successful, as well as to provide for Gaunt's physical and spiritual comfort wherever he was, required the constant activity of three hundred officials and the skins of ten thousand sheep for parchment. Being a warrior of Gaunt's stature was complicated and expensive.

◦〜◦

In spite of all the money expended on a military campaign, in spite of all the logistical and administrative efforts of Gaunt's officials, the actual war could be a failure, the results not only negligible but miserable.

It is very wrong to associate England's role in the Hundred Years' War with incessant glory. After the Black Prince won two great battles early in the war, English arms never again enjoyed an unqualified victory until Henry V's triumph at Agincourt in 1415, and thirty-six years after that battle, the English had been driven from nearly all of France.

We think of John of Gaunt with his large armies—as many as fifteen thousand soldiers. We think of his many years of careful training under his brother. We think of his personal military skill at fighting from horseback and with lance and sword. We think of his gorgeous armor and his immensely strong body enabling him to endure long marches on horseback. We think of him as a traveling man, capable of traversing long distances in bad weather as well as good. But the underside of Gaunt's wars was defeat, hunger, waste of resources, and humiliation.

In 1373 Gaunt set out on a grand march through the middle of France. Six months later he had traversed a huge circle, never getting the French to come to organized battle and devastating vast stretches of the French countryside. During this time, Gaunt lost nearly half his army of fifteen thousand men to disease and hunger and thoroughly wasted the precious tax-raised resources Edward III and Parliament had given him.

Of the 15,000 men who marched out of Calais with such high hopes, only 8,000 were left, and of these only half were still mounted.

The rest had perished, few by the hand of the enemy, almost all of the hardships suffered in that last fearful stage of the journey, from Clermont to Mur-de-Barrez. It was a pitiable condition to which one of the best equipped of English armies had been reduced . . .

From Calais to Bordeaux through the heart of France, the Duke had led his army, wasting cornland and vineyard, burning and putting to ransom château, manor and village. For five months he had offered the enemy whose lands he insulted constant challenge of battle, and that challenge had been constantly refused. From start to finish no opposition worth the name had been offered, no army had dared to meet him in the field.

This seeming triumph obscured, in the minds of the invaded, at any rate, if not also of the invaders, the utter futility of the whole proceeding. No military result had been achieved. An incalculable amount of misery, it is true, had been inflicted on the French peasantry, but Edward III had been brought no nearer to the throne of the Valois by his son's efforts. And this campaign without battles, upon which so much had been built, this great military promenade, so far from achieving any positive result, in truth amounted to a disaster to English arms. The Duke's point-to-point race across France had cost an English army.

S. Armitage-Smith

Gaunt was so depressed by his miserable failure in 1373 that he retired to his country estate at Pontefract in the north for ten months to brood over the causes of his great setback. He emerged from retirement wanting to be an ambassador rather than a general. He played a leading part in the peace negotiations with the King of France, Charles V, at Calais. In the end they were unsuccessful because the French government wanted most of the lands back, particularly in the Aquitaine in the south, and the English government, embarrassed by having spent parliamentary taxes with so little result, would not concede a major withdrawal.

It was not until 1386 that Gaunt again launched a major continental expedition, this time against Castile, although with a much smaller army at his back than in 1373. This expedition too failed to achieve its goal, although Gaunt got a big pot of money out of it, an indication that by then he was more pliable Renaissance prince than impractical medieval warrior, and was satisfied to slake his greed rather than his thirst for glory.

We must not forget, however, how physically tough it was to be a general in the Hundred Years' War. It required travel on horseback over long distances in inclement weather; it required enormous physical strength to make these travels and then, often, to fight immediately hand-to-hand in battle. It also required a surprising amount of strategic planning and tactical leadership.

The life of a general in Gaunt's time was more closely akin to that of a professional football player than to that of a modern-day general. It is amazing that Gaunt was still trying to lead an army at the age of forty-six, his body wracked with cuts, bruises, and disease, his mind preoccupied with family cares, estate management, and recollected disappointments. What needs to be stressed about Gaunt is that he was a man of unusual physical strength and enormous personal courage.

Though he did not care in the least about French peasants, Gaunt cared for the thousands of cavalry and infantry who were under his command. He had to, or he could not have conducted a military campaign. Gaunt had empathy for these lords, knights, and foot soldiers. He knew how they felt, knew what their needs were. They were a political entity on the move.

Medieval states made war, but war also made medieval

states. The organization, the logistics of feeding and arming, the chain of command, the disbursement of wages and the keeping of records, all these governmental and political functions were involved in fighting the Hundred Years' War.

The discipline within the ranks, the emotional joining together of thousands of soldiers under a common leadership, these were political functions that had to be harnessed and controlled. Gaunt benefited from the growth of the Plantagenet state. But making war on an extensive scale also solidified and entrenched state functions, especially taxation and the recruitment, transportation, training, and supplying of military personnel. Making war also gave the royal government experience in organizing and bribing allies and in issuing propaganda communiques.

❧

In the making of the fourteenth-century warrior aristocracy, what counted was not only what was actually done on the battlefield and how the aristocrats organized their resources for war. What also shaped the way in which the aristocracy was perceived was the heroic image of the great nobility communicated by the romantic literature of the time. The elaborate dress and lifestyle of the aristocracy conformed more easily to the heroic image than to any actual performance. This made the romantic image of the high aristocrat all the more important.

Romantic mythmaking and literary traditions played a

significant role in how someone at the apex of the social hierarchy like Gaunt was perceived. He was seen through the haze of romantic idealism.

There were three literary traditions at work in Gaunt's time that shaped the heroic image of the warrior aristocracy. Works within these traditions were transmitted both orally and in physical form. The poems were recited to the accompaniment of music at dinners in noble, gentry, and merchant households. But the poems were also written out in manuscripts, some in curled-up rolls and some in codices (bound books). In the second half of the fourteenth century these literary manuscripts came to be heavily illustrated, and their imagery was thereby communicated even more vividly.

The three literary traditions centered on Charlemagne and his family ("the Matter of France"); King Arthur and Queen Guinevere and their court ("the Matter of Britain"); and Alexander the Great (the Alexandrine cycle, stories about the great hero of the ancient world). Charlemagne (d. A.D. 814) and Alexander (d. 323 B.C.) were certainly historical figures. King Arthur (fl. c. A.D. 520) probably was an actual person. However, the portrayal of these leaders in romantic literature was heavily altered to suit heroic ideals and poetic themes.

Alexander the Great became in the Alexandrine romances a fantasy figure. He not only conquered the eastern Mediterranean and Western Asia (as was historically true), he marched to the end of the world and there prayed to the sun and moon. He entered a glass submarine and examined the ocean floor. He aimed to bring together East and West. He was superman.

Charlemagne was a white-bearded Christian emperor who fought—unsuccessfully—against the dark Muslim Moors in Spain. He and his family suffered a great tragedy when Charlemagne's nephew Count Roland, heading the rear guard of the French army as it withdrew through the Pyrenees, was overcome and killed by the more numerous Muslims because Roland was ashamed to blow his horn and summon Charlemagne's help. This episode has historical foundation.

There are at least two subtraditions within the Matter of Britain. One involves the sexual love triangle of Arthur, Guinevere, and Arthur's most admirable knight, Lancelot— still a favorite Hollywood plot. All we know historically about King Arthur is that he was of Celtic-Roman origin and he led the Celtic Britons in two decades of holding back the onslaught of the invading Anglo-Saxon Germans. The love triangle was something developed by twelfth-century writers. Its plot is essentially the same as that of another twelfth-century romance, the story of Tristan and Isolde. The idea of a young noble having an affair with the king's wife was obviously appealing.

The other subtradition in the Matter of Britain, or Arthurian cycle, is the search for the Holy Grail by one or more knightly members of the Court of the Round Table. These two traditions opened the way for deeper probing—

into the psychology of gender relationships and the meaning of personal purity, which allows for the finding of the Grail. Here the Matter of Britain provides surface plots for deep psychological and religious insight.

John of Gaunt and Edward the Black Prince were seen in their own time through the sensibility communicated by these literary traditions. Gaunt and Edward were bound to appear more gigantic and exciting when viewed through the scrim of these ideals of romantic heroism.

༺∞∞༻

I remember being admonished in the 1950s, in Joseph Strayer's Princeton doctoral seminar on medieval politics and society, against giving any historical value to the romantic literary and artistic traditions of the later Middle Ages. Stick to tax rolls and property records and administrative letters—there was the truth, we were told. But how Gaunt was perceived by minds steeped in these romantic traditions is also part of history.

Like Alexander the Great, Gaunt would do fantastic and seemingly superhuman things. Like Charlemagne, he was a wise, good-hearted Christian leader. Like King Arthur and the knights of the Round Table, he would define human love and act upon that definition. His relative purity would allow him to reach the highest goals. These were the ways romance culture constituted a prism through which Gaunt was viewed.

Minds immersed in the Alexandrine cycle, the Matter of

France, or the Matter of Britain could see Gaunt within the frame and color of these stories generated by the romantic genre. As for now, choose the movie you want to see—an Errol Flynn swashbuckler from the 1930s, a PBS historical documentary, or a Martin Scorsese quasi realistic film set perilously at some moment in the past, and you can place Gaunt in any of the frames.

The three great romantic literary traditions—the Alexandrine, the Matter of France, and the Arthurian—communicate different political messages. Alexander, blessed by the gods, does pretty much what he wants and vanquishes all human opposition. Charlemagne has the reputation of a great warrior, but he is old and increasingly feeble. He relies on the younger members of his family. Arthur is altogether a weak character. He cannot control his wayward wife; he is betrayed by his favorite vassal, Lancelot. Arthur is something of a mediocre chairman of the board. It is young Sir Gallahad, the pure one, who finds the Grail, not stumbling Arthur.

Gaunt wanted to be Alexander. In fact, he was more like Charlemagne and Arthur. Yet the shining romantic image stayed with him, both as he saw himself and as others saw him. To say that Gaunt less resembled Alexander, with his insatiable ambition and unlimited power, than he did Charlemagne and Arthur, embedded in communal restraints and dependent on others, is one way of distinguishing the politics of the ancient world from that of the Middle Ages.

Heroism is the reflection of a social system, a way of understanding the world. It means the personification of power. The troubles of society and, by implication, individuals' problems could and would be solved by a hero, a strong man of noble ideals and the best intentions who would dominate and destroy the enemy, the force of evil in whatever form it took.

That is why the story of Alexander the Great was so popular. That is why the English poet Geoffrey Chaucer could write, "The story of Alexander is so common / That every person that has understanding / Has heard somewhat or all of his good fortune." There was deep satisfaction in contemplating a man who overcame all enemies from Greece to India. His opponents tried to put him at a disadvantage with large fleets of ships and troops of elephants, but to no avail: Alexander overcame them all.

English society and culture of the late fourteenth century wanted John of Gaunt to be their Alexander. He seemed to have the qualifications—wealth, physical strength, royal lineage, literacy, powerful heterosexuality. But one thing Gaunt did not have was Alexander's incredible luck. In that way, Gaunt closely resembled the two other great heroes of fourteenth-century sensibility, Arthur and Charlemagne. He was a hero, but a flawed and unfortunate one. He was more the representative of his world than its savior.

CHAPTER SIX

Spain

IN 1387 THE ENVOYS of the King of Castile in Spain, Juan I, caught up with John of Gaunt at Trancosa in northern Portugal. Gaunt was on his way south to visit his daughter Philippa, who had a year earlier married the King of Portugal, João I, and was now pregnant. Gaunt continued south to the Portuguese court. He assigned Sir Thomas Percy, from a great family in northern England, and a trusted councilor, to negotiate with the Castilian envoys according to guidelines Gaunt laid down.

The most important requirement was for Juan I to make a financial settlement with Gaunt. Eventually the negotiators decided on a payment that would be the equivalent of $1 billion in our money, plus $10 million a year for life. Of course, only a fraction of this money was ever paid out to Gaunt, as was typical of a medieval diplomatic subvention. But it was enough for Gaunt to fulfill his part of the bargain and leave

Spain, giving up the claim to the Castilian throne he had acquired through his wife Constance.

It was not a great concession on Gaunt's part. Since he had married the Castilian princess in 1369, Gaunt had claimed the throne. He minted coins and issued documents as King of Castile. He was the legitimate ruler, even though the lords, knights, and burghers of Castile preferred an illegitimate line. It was only in 1386, during a hiatus in the Hundred Years' War with France, that Gaunt had the opportunity to invade Spain through Galicia, on the sea in the northwest corner of Spain. He made an alliance with King João of Portugal and bonded it with Philippa's marriage, and together Gaunt and the Portuguese king advanced on Castile.

They were easily repulsed by Juan I, principally because Gaunt's army was too small and was furthermore diminished by plague. The funding for Gaunt's army contributed by his nephew King Richard II of England and by Parliament was miserly, and Gaunt had dipped into his own vast resources to outfit an army of English and French mercenaries for the invasion. But it was not enough.

John of Gaunt had sufficient private resources to put together a large army, which alongside the forces of João of Portugal could probably have gained the Castilian throne, for Gaunt was the richest man in Europe. But in 1387 Gaunt was already forty-seven years old, elderly by the standards of the Middle Ages, when the life expectancy of a male member of the aristocracy was forty years.

Gaunt had been engaged in warfare since he was an adolescent, and his body was wearing down. He had many children. He had to think of his progeny and their inheritances. He could risk only a small part of his vast wealth in the Spanish venture. Meanwhile, the Castilian king was well supplied with soldiers. Two centuries of Christian reconquest of Spain from the Muslims had left a powerful military legacy among the Castilian nobility.

Gaunt decided that the road to victory in Spain would be a long one. He decided to fold his tents, take as much money as he could get from Juan I, and go back to England, where his young nephew King Richard II was getting on poorly with some of the aristocracy and could use Lancaster's help.

Gaunt was a Plantagenet, a member of the dynasty that had ruled England since 1154. He shared many characteristics with other male Plantagenets. He had reddish-blond hair, wore a trimmed beard, was a great fighter in hand-to-hand combat, and had a fierce temper. His height, five feet eight inches, was above average. Like other members of his family, Gaunt had an extravagant lifestyle in terms of houses, clothes, jewels, horses, cuisine, and wine. His sport was hunting, aided by specially bred falcons. Gaunt, like all the Plantagenets, saw himself as belonging to a very small international elite of blue bloods, among whom the only full social equals were the King of France and some of his children.

There was enough intermarriage between the Plantagenets and the French royal family for Edward III, who came to the English throne in 1327 as a minor, to make a claim to the French crown ten years into his reign. This precipitated what we know as the Hundred Years' War, in which the western third of France was devastated at the hands of English mercenaries.

It was only during a long period of truce with France in the late fourteenth century that Gaunt finally had the opportunity and royal permission to pursue his claim to the Castilian throne and invade Spain. Nothing politically significant came of that. But Gaunt left two daughters as his legacy in the Iberian peninsula. Not only did his daughter Philippa by his first wife, the great heiress Blanche, marry the King of Portugal, but his daughter Catalina by his second wife, Constance, married the son of Juan I of Castile in 1387 as part of the peacemaking process. There was one child born to the marriage of Catalina and the Castilian heir, and so Lancastrian blood entered into the royal family of Castile.

The marriage of Philippa and João of Portugal founded an important dynasty. One of their sons, Prince Henrique, organized expeditions down the west coast of Africa to find gold and bring back black slaves. He was called Henry the Navigator by nineteenth-century historians. He is regarded as an important name in the beginnings of European commercial imperialism. The marriage of Gaunt's daughter and the King of Portugal inaugurated close economic and political ties between England and Portugal that endured into the nineteenth century.

Port and Portuguese sherry are still favorite drinks of the British upper classes. If you dine with the dons in Oxford and Cambridge colleges, after dinner you will be offered, along with cigars and chocolates, the opportunity to pour yourself a small glass of port. Port was imported into England from Lisbon. While enjoying this drink, all port drinkers in England should think of John of Gaunt, Duke of Lancaster. It is a legacy of his ill-fated expedition to Spain in 1386–1387.

A second legacy to the peninsula—for good and bad—was his Portuguese grandson Prince Henry, born from the union of the King of Portugal and Gaunt's daughter Philippa. The Portuguese royal family knew they could never conquer the large and rich Castilian kingdom. Instead, led by Prince Henry, they looked south to the west coast of Africa. They founded the black slave trade.

The black slaves were used domestically in Portugal and its colony in the Azores, and were traded off to Spanish Christians and to Muslims in Turkish lands. By the third decade of the sixteenth century, the Portuguese were carving out huge plantations in Brazil, with their African slaves providing the labor. At this time Christian theologians were still disputing whether the African slaves had souls. The Church eventually decided in the affirmative, but the bishops and friars did not question the institution of slavery.

The slave trade was the most lucrative avenue of commerce and industry before the eighteenth century, and the Portuguese monopolized it until challenged by the Dutch and English slave traders in the seventeenth century. It was the Portuguese who initially provided the black slaves for the vast Spanish holdings in Central and South America. Historians have estimated that at least 20 percent of the slaves transported from the west coast of Africa never made it alive across the Atlantic in the holds of the slave traders' ships.

What Prince Henry the Navigator, Gaunt's grandson, had begun was built upon by Portuguese admirals. In 1498 Vasco da Gama rounded the Cape of Good Hope and reached the west coast of India, opening up a new European trade route to the Orient and inaugurating Europe's eastward commercial expansion. The Portuguese established a colonial entrepôt on the west coast of India, Goa, which they held on to until the 1960s. The cloths and spices imported from Goa added an Indian flavor to the Muslim and Jewish base of Portuguese culture, cuisine, and fashion.

Gaunt would have been happy to know that the diplomatic marriage of his daughter Philippa to the King of Portugal would have such a world-changing impact. His grandson Prince Henry the Navigator was in the Plantagenet mold, enterprising and ruthless, and set about conquering as much of the world as possible. So began the European and subsequently the English domination of the world.

ⵢⵟⵟⵡⵙ

The Anglo-French aristocracy referred to Castile—along with the kingdom of Aragon and León in the eastern part of

the peninsula—as Iberia. To the Muslim and Jewish populations there it was Andalusia, a land of wealth, learning, and
enchantment. In the early eighth century the Moors, a mixture of Arab and Berber peoples recently converted to Islam,
had crossed the Strait of Gibraltar from Africa and invaded
the old kingdom of Spain. They defeated the Spanish Christian princes and drove them and some of their soldiers into
the foothills of the Pyrenees up north.

The Muslim majority of Andalusia, eventually 6 million
people, was joined by 1 million Jews, some of them from
families that went back to Roman times, some newly immigrated from north Africa and Egypt. The Muslims and Jews
created a prosperous society, linked by international trade
routes and family corporations with the eastern part of the
Mediterranean and beyond the Middle East with India.

The Muslim-Jewish cities like Córdoba, Lisbon, Barcelona,
and Burgos became centers of learning as well as centers of
commerce and small-scale industry. Around A.D.1000, church
scholars from France crossed the mountains to study philosophy, medicine, and mathematics in the schools of Andalusia.
The Muslim and Jewish scholars had available to them Arabic
translations of Greek philosophical and scientific writings.

The cuisine of Andalusia was famous throughout Europe,
and was much more advanced than that in Christian countries. The Andalusians used olive oil as their cooking fat
instead of lard, which was the cooking base in Christian countries. The Andalusians' cooked fish and meats were heavily

spiced with condiments imported from Egypt and India, including saffron, black pepper, fennel, and curry mixtures. Lamb was the Andalusians' favorite meat. The roast leg of lamb we eat today is close to the medieval Andalusian recipe.

Cod, hake, and sardines were popular fish in Andalusia. When you open a tin of spiced Portuguese or Spanish sardines today, you are taking a culinary trip into the Muslim-Jewish world of Andalusia.

The Muslim Arabs and the Jews developed genres in music and wrote an impressive body of love poetry, some of it homoerotic. The early work of the twelfth-century Jewish poet Judah ha-Levi is remarkably homoerotic.

In the twelfth century the Christian reconquest of Iberia began, with the Christian princes and their soldiers moving south from their mountain redoubts. With the help of French crusaders, by the end of the thirteenth century the Christian reconquest was almost complete, except for the small Arab state of Granada in the south.

Led by the Dominican and Franciscan friars, the Iberian churches brought great pressure on the Muslims and Jews to convert to the Roman Catholic religion. By 1350 perhaps half of the Muslim and Jewish populations had accepted baptism into the Church, with varying degrees of sincerity.

Many mosques were turned into Christian churches; their architecture is still admired today. But the Muslims and the Jews continued to exert a heavy influence on Iberia. Commerce and urban life, skilled craftsmanship, big barrels of olive oil and red wine, music, poetry, art, and cuisine reflected the five centuries of Muslim and Jewish hegemony.

Spain and Portugal were admired in northern Europe, as was the Iberian Peninsula's mild climate. The French monarchy took a great interest in Iberia, married into the Christian ruling families there, and formed political alliances with Iberian principalities, especially Castile. In the 1370s combined Castilian and French fleets raided the south coast of England.

There was a good reason why the English Plantagenet family wanted to grab a large foothold on the Iberian Peninsula. The richest part of Spain was the kingdom of Aragon and León. Aragon, on the east coast, with its great port of Barcelona—commercially connected to the golden land of Sicily, breadbasket of Italy since Roman times—was especially prized by the European kings. Aragon was too wealthy and militarily strong to attack, and, being on the Iberian east coast, it was not easily accessible from France or England.

Castile, a mostly rural area famed for the quality of its wool, was accessible and was more vulnerable than fabled Aragon. Castile was highly prized by the English and French royal families. Any country replete with Arabs and Jews had close association with fabulous wealth, there to be taken by an invader.

☙

As early as 1346 Edward III had tried to forge a dynastic alliance with the King of Castile through marriage of his daughter Joan to the heir to the Castilian throne. But thanks to the Black Death, poor Joan's fate awaited her in Bordeaux, on the journey to Spain.

In 1371 Gaunt tried to pursue his family's Spanish ambitions by marrying Constance, daughter of Pedro I, known as Pedro the Cruel, and the presumed heiress to the Castilian throne. But when she was pushed aside by her illegitimate cousin, Henry of Trastámara, Henry gained the loyalty of the nobility and towns. They found Henry more accommodating to their interests.

Gaunt spent five years of his life fighting in Spain. Two years were spent alongside the Black Prince, whose Spanish wars ultimately achieved nothing. Three years were spent in Iberia fighting for Constance's claim to the Castilian throne before Gaunt gave up for a pot of money.

What attracted Gaunt to Spain was the warmth of the country and the richness of its agriculture. The orange groves and the droves of sheep offered a powerful attraction, as did Iberia's thriving commerce with the Mediterranean and the skill and capital of its diverse population, especially the Muslims and Jews.

When the Sephardic Jews numbering 200,000 were expelled from Iberia in the early sixteenth century, they held on, into the twentieth century, to their distinctive liturgy, their language (a Hebrew-Spanish dialect), and their beautiful dress and exquisite cuisine, all too precious to abandon. The Plantagenets wanted in on this sweet, sunny land, its Roman and Oriental traditions embedded in its fruitful soil.

But would Gaunt have been happy as King of Castile? It is hard to say. He never learned the language. He would have found the political strength of the nobility and the fierce independence of the towns challenging.

He would have had trouble accommodating himself to Spanish food. Chicken, paella, thick, highly flavored lamb stew, and spiced fish after English barbecue and meat pies? It was not a bad idea to go home with all that cash. England was a simpler, underflavored world.

CHAPTER SEVEN

The Church

J OHN OF GAUNT'S FIRST commitment was to his family. The people he loved most were his mother the Queen, his elder brother the Black Prince, and the first and third of his wives. His second commitment was to the chivalric code and remained so until his death. He enjoyed fighting on the battlefield and was an inveterate sponsor of and participant in tournaments. His behavior toward aristocratic women showed his recognition of courtly love. He moved readily and eagerly within the circumscribed but civilized lifestyle of the Anglo-French aristocracy.

Gaunt's third commitment was to the management of his vast estates, which lay mostly in northern England and in Aquitaine. He employed a skillful and tightfisted group of managers for his English estates, which produced revenues of around $500 million a year.

Gaunt also had a commitment to what historians call his "affinity," or retainers, the thousands of lesser nobility, gentry, and mercenaries bound in their loyalty to him by one form of contract (such as indenture) or another. Many of them wore the Lancastrian badge, and they fought for him, if they were able-bodied and he summoned them to France, Spain, or Scotland. His obligation to them involved grants of land, sharing of war booty, helping to arrange marriages, and support in the law courts, especially in civil (property) disputes.

Some of his affinity also received government jobs, such as sheriff, tax collector, justice of the peace (a local magistrate), and as members of Parliament. But careful research has shown that Gaunt did not pursue bureaucratic rewards for his affinity as much as he could have. It was part of his nature to limit the use he would make of his position as a royal prince. He was conscious that maximizing the advantages of his status could arouse resentment among the nobility and commoners alike.

In addition to pursuing all these activities, Gaunt became involved with religious leaders and groups, activist peasants, Parliament, and his unfortunate nephew Richard II. Given his status, wealth, and visibility, these involvements are not surprising and in many instances were unavoidable. But Gaunt's involvement with the heretical don, preacher, and writer John Wyclif for about a decade was his own choice and shows a disposition, for a time, toward radical religious ideas.

A papal inquisition was a special Church court set up to prosecute religious heretics, including those who had strayed from the Roman Catholic faith and had set up subversive counterchurches. In the thirteenth and fourteenth centuries papal inquisitions were frequently at work in southern France, where there was a massive heretical movement, the Albigensians.

A papal inquisition had never operated in England, partly because Henry II had kept out of the country the inquisitorial judges mandated to discover and punish religious heretics and partly because after his reign no heretics were visible in England. Before 1350 the classic law of doctrinal error remained active in southern France, the Rhine Valley, and northern Italy. If there was a popular heretical movement in England during the thirteenth century, it had to have functioned deep underground, and historians have not discovered it.

A heretical movement finally began in England in the 1360s, led by John Wyclif (d. 1384). Wyclif was an ambitious and disgruntled Oxford don from the lower gentry, the source of most medieval academics. He taught assiduously and also wrote very learned and highly polemical theological treatises in both Latin and English. He preached frequently in the university church.

Wyclif seems in the beginning to have been motivated by hostility to and jealousy of the friars, Franciscan and Dominican. As a secular priest (not a monk or friar) and college don, he did not have the financial help that the religious orders provided for their members studying at Oxford.

Although Wyclif eventually obtained enough Church preferment to finance his advanced studies, he had already become an embittered extremist, and in the Oxford philosophy faculty he found no mentor to get him to moderate his views.

Wyclif was philosophically a Platonist, or, as an adherent of Platonism was then called, a "realist." For Wyclif, only pure ideas had reality, i.e., permanence, integrity, legitimacy. Compared with the pure idea of a church, the English Church of his day was far from ideal. Any material involvement of bishops and friars detracted from their legitimacy, in his view.

Wyclif was a brilliant polemicist and he had a masterly, encyclopedic knowledge of the Scriptures. It was not easy to debate with him, although several dons tried. In his own eyes, Wyclif never lost a debate. He was a charismatic figure in the academic world and his fame began to spread to wider circles.

Wyclif gained further attention by propounding the doctrine of *dominium,* which had been articulated by Marsilius of Padua and William of Occam early in the century. According to this doctrine, since the state had sovereign power, it could and should divest the churchmen of their lands. Marsilius and Occam were not obscure figures. They were prominent professors. Marsilius taught at the University of Paris. In a long treatise he contended that only complete domination by the state over the church allowed for social peace and stability.

Occam was a philosophical genius who was a member of the radical wing of his order, the Franciscans, at Oxford. He adhered to the doctrine of apostolic poverty, which advocated that churchmen give up their property and live as mendicants. This revolutionary doctrine was condemned as heresy by the papacy in 1322.

Inevitably both Marsilius and Occam fell afoul of Church authorities. They found refuge at the court of the Holy Roman Emperor, Lewis IV of Bavaria.

Occam and Wyclif belonged to opposing philosophical schools. Occam was a nominalist, or anti-Platonist; Wyclif a realist, or Platonist. Yet in spite of contrasting philosophical assumptions, Occam and Wyclif ended up with similar antiecclesiastical conclusions. For Occam the idea of the Church as a universal institution had no intellectual merit. For Wyclif, the Church fell far short of its institutional ideal and therefore had lost its moral authority.

Wyclif was a brilliant and immensely learned man who translated his personal contempt for most churchmen of his day into radical ideas. All three—Marsilius, Occam, and Wyclif—looked to the power of the state as the means of social salvation and the route to enhancement of their unfulfilling academic careers.

Wyclif became more radical as time went on, attacking the Church's sacramental system and the doctrine of transubstantiation, the theoretical basis for the sacrament of the Eucharist and for the Mass. He denounced the papacy as evil.

Some of Wyclif's disciples translated the Bible into English for literate workers and gentry, something the more conservative bishops regarded as a subversive move. Wyclif's graduate students went out of Oxford into the countryside and preached his radical doctrines; they were called Lollards.

About five hundred pages of Lollard writings have survived. These pages are written in English. The Lollard writers call for "reformation of the holy church of England." The pope is "a blasphemer and Lucifer and anti-Christ." The contemporary priesthood is "not the priesthood for which Christ ordained his apostles." The Church is "full of idolatry."

Such inflammatory statements reflect a growing unease among the English people about the rectitude of the clergy. They also reflect the postadolescent radicalism among graduate students in all times and places. Wyclif capitalized on these feelings, articulating them into elaborate theological treatises, mostly written in Latin.

University teachers were allowed a wide doctrinal latitude by the medieval Church on what they communicated orally. It was when they wrote down and circulated their radical ideas that the authorities became alarmed. Yet despite his radical writings, most of the English bishops preferred to ignore Wyclif; they had no tradition of persecuting heretics, as there was in France. But William Courtenay, Bishop of London (later Archbishop of Canterbury), was a hardliner. He got permission from the papacy to set up a court of inquisition.

Wyclif sometimes preached at the royal court. John of Gaunt had become acquainted with him there. Gaunt offered the rebellious don patronage and protection. He arranged for Wyclif to be appointed to a diplomatic mission to Belgium. As Britain's leading landowner, Gaunt undoubtedly was attracted to the doctrine of *dominium* in Wyclif's teaching, since it legitimated royal and aristocratic expropriation of Church property.

The Black Death and the malaise it caused had set off novel spiritual quests, and this also affected Gaunt, as it did others. He wanted to give Wyclif a hearing. When Wyclif was at last forced to appear before an inquisitorial court in London headed by Bishop Courtenay, Gaunt set off a riot.

Bishop Courtenay was popular among the street people in London. That did not prevent Gaunt at one point from threatening to drag him out by the hair of his head. The inquisitorial court broke up in confusion and Wyclif was not condemned.

Wyclif was never again brought to trial by the Church authorities, although some of his Lollard followers, so summoned, either recanted or received very moderate punishment. This was not France. After supporting Wyclif for a decade, however, Gaunt separated from him. Pursuing the religious quest fashionable at the time, Gaunt had become enamored of the Carmelites, a small and very strict order of friars. The Duke switched his religious patronage to the Carmelites, moving from radical to conservative extremes.

But Wyclif was not forsaken by people in high circles. He was given a rich parish, to which he retired from Oxford, and he spent his remaining years turning out more heretical treatises. His doctrines were similar to that of the radical Protestantism in the late sixteenth century out of which the Congregational and Baptist communities developed.

Wyclif's teaching affected another European country: Bohemia (now the Czech Republic). Gaunt's nephew Richard II married Anne of Bohemia, and Wyclif's writings migrated from the English royal court to Prague. Wyclif's doctrine thereby inspired the rise of a great heretical movement in Bohemia under the early leadership of John Hus. After a prolonged struggle, the Hussites formed the first Protestant state in Europe in the fifteenth century, antedating Lutheran Germany.

There was a definite connection between the Lancastrian court and the Lollards, starting with Gaunt's early support of Wyclif. Gaunt's son Henry IV (r. 1399–1413) discovered, a half-dozen years into his reign, that perhaps a dozen knights in the royal court, members of the highest stratum of the gentry, were supporters of the Lollard preachers. The King brought down upon the "Lollard knights" all the power of Church and state. Henry IV was convinced the Lollard knights were subversive.

Their response was to organize a bizarre insurrection in the early months of Henry V's reign. The insurrection, led by a prominent mercenary and military hero, Sir John Oldcastle, was put down handily and Oldcastle was hunted down. It was alarming to both Henry IV and Henry V that Lollardy had penetrated into the highest ranks of the gentry.

The persecution of the Lollard knights seems to have stopped this threat. There is no doubt that the Lollard knights were religious idealists, true believers. But after the government had suppressed them, the Lollards retreated to country districts in the north, where they lived mainly among peasant families.

When Henry VIII separated England from Rome in the 1530s, the remaining tiny group of Lollards joined up with the Lutherans, whose pamphlets were imported from the Continent in herring barrels. By 1420 the Lollards had become like the Amish in the United States today. They were a very small group of hardworking farmers in the north for whom Wyclif's teachings had become a bonding identity.

How different it would have been if Gaunt had persisted in his early public and private support of Wyclif. He could have played the decisive role that Frederick the Wise, the Elector of Saxony, took in Martin Luther's lifetime in the founding of the Lutheran Church, a role—even though Luther and his aristocratic patron never met face-to-face—that was almost as great as that of Luther himself.

The younger Gaunt was looking for some kind of novel spiritual commitment in the fearsome age of the Black Death when faith healing was not having much success. Gaunt could have become a devotee of the mystics who were appearing all over the country. But the mystics' message was too amorphous for him and their prescribed contemplative lifestyle too detached and static for a man of Lancaster's military activity and sex drive.

For a time Wyclif appealed to Gaunt. The Oxford don's powerful preaching, his immense learning, and his courageous onslaught upon the religious establishment as well as his justification for expropriation of Church lands by the state and aristocracy—all this appealed to Gaunt. But the furious ramblings of this quarrelsome and ambitious professor grated on Gaunt's refined aristocratic disposition.

Wyclif's scurvy graduate students, the Lollards, preaching in market and town, brought home to Gaunt the potential serious consequences of the Wyclifite movement. Perhaps Gaunt got wind of the spread of Lollardy to court gentry.

In any event, Gaunt drew back from being at the center of a social and religious maelstrom. He found an uncontroversial and satisfying outlet for his spiritual quest: his support and patronage of the austere Carmelite order of friars. This kind of moderate religious gesture had been embraced defensively by the great families for centuries. This conservative spiritual behavior and break with Wyclif fit in well with the mind-set of the grandest and richest knight in Christendom.

In this respect Gaunt was clearly a man of the Middle Ages rather than of the early modern world. Religion was a matter for private cultivation through his personal devotions and his patronage of the Carmelites. Religion was, after all, not a public, social, or political matter, not a mechanism for transforming culture.

This was the Catholic way. The medieval aristocracy thought of religion as a deeply personal thing, and gave churchmen resources to pursue their mission of converting and comforting souls. Medieval aristocrats like Gaunt did not want to see religion as an entry point for transforming the structure of society and government.

It is remarkable that a younger Gaunt was tempted by Wyclif's revolutionary vision. But as Gaunt aged, he returned to the traditional aristocratic dichotomy of religion and the world. If society and government needed restructuring, the aristocracy would do it, soothed by the chanting of traditional monks like the Carmelites.

Back in the late eleventh century a group of cardinals and monks led by Pope Gregory VII (d. 1085) had sought to unite the Church and the world and restructure society under papal leadership. The aristocracy of the time defied the Gregorian reformers and prevailed over them. Wyclif was antipapist, but he too wanted to integrate the Church and society, or so Gaunt came to suspect. This kind of radical idealism could not be allowed to prevail, in Gaunt's mature judgment.

⁊⁊⁊

Historians have called the Wyclifite movement the Premature Reformation. In the end it was mostly unsuccessful, but it was not premature. In Gaunt's lifetime English society was ready for a reformation, for several reasons.

First, the papacy had disgraced itself and had acquired a bad reputation in England. Since the first decade of the fourteenth century the popes, always now Frenchmen, had resided in Avignon on the Rhone River and had become closely associated with the French monarchy. There was a popular national antipapal feeling in England, compounded by heavy papal taxation of the English clergy.

What was particularly grating in England was the papacy's persistent and partly successful effort to control appointments in the English Church or cathedral canons and priests in the larger and more lucrative parishes. The appointees were almost invariably Italians or Frenchmen and usually they did not appear in England to do their work. Instead they would appoint an Englishman as a vicar who actually did the job. Meanwhile the Italian or French appointee would collect a significant share of the income afforded by the ecclesiastical office. What was on the surface a dispute about Church organization and discipline was inflamed by nationalist feeling against foreigners.

The ecclesiastical situation became worse in 1378, when the minority of Italian cardinals went back to Rome and elected a pope. The French majority among the cardinals continued to reside in Avignon and elected their own pope. There were now two contending popes in Christendom. This scandalous Great Schism lasted until 1417.

A second ground for a reformation in England had been laid by the socially radical preaching of the Franciscans. In the early fourteenth century the Pope had condemned the radical wing of the Franciscan order, but the radicals' egalitarian ideas had already penetrated into Christian culture. Although Wyclif was at odds with the order, purged of radicalism by his day, he built upon the leftist antipapal and antihierarchical teachings of the now condemned Spiritual Franciscans.

A third reason for a potential reformation in England came from the widespread criticism of the clergy as corrupt and ineffective. The older monasteries in particular had become very rich land corporations and contributed little to society. The monks' daily consumption of an enormous amount of food was legendary: the fat, lazy monk became the staple of a growing anticlerical literature. Geoffrey Chaucer contributed to this anticlerical literature in *The Canterbury Tales*. His descriptions of the Prioress, Monk, Friar, Summoner, and Pardoner are all detrimental to the image of the Church. Only the lowly Parson represents the true spirit of Christianity.

What was lacking in the highly combustible religious ambience in late-fourteenth-century England was secular political leadership to break with Rome and open the floodgates to a reformation. Henry VIII's break with Rome in the 1530s was to provide that opening. But in fourteenth-century England, Gaunt's abandonment of Wyclif after supporting him early on precluded the reformation. It was Gaunt's turning away from the radical professor that stopped a religious revolution.

The ingredients of Protestantism in 1370 lay deep in English culture and society. These ingredients could have led to a substantially reformed Church in England. But the extremism of the later Wyclif and the lack of discipline among his Lollard followers made it impossible for Gaunt to continue to cooperate with them. Thus the Wyclifites lost the political leadership they needed to foment a reformation 150 years before Henry VIII.

There was a time in the late eleventh and twelfth centuries when England's bishops and abbots, under strong leadership from Rome, asserted the Church's identity and made a claim for autonomy. By Gaunt's time, those days were long gone. The Church in England had come completely under the domination of the royal government and the great aristocratic families. Parliament even passed a law (which was not observed) prohibiting churchmen in England from communicating with the papacy without permission of the royal government.

The "Babylonian Captivity" of the papacy in Avignon and then from 1378 to 1417 the Great Schism, with popes in both Avignon and Rome, severely damaged the Church's image among the lay population. But even aside from this disaster, the bishops, abbots, and heads of religious orders in England had come to adopt a national rather than international perspective. They were dependent on and subservient to the royal government and the aristocracy. Therefore when Wyclif and his disciples attempted a radical reform of the Church, they made very little progress because they lacked the necessary secular support among the elite.

That the Wyclifite movement was antipapal cut Wyclif and his followers off from the support of whatever remained of the Church as an international institution. The Wyclifite movement for reform could only be a national one.

⟨∾⟩

In the late nineteenth century and the early decades of the twentieth century, Protestant and secular historians spoke of the "decline of the medieval Church." They are less inclined to do so today because, while the Latin Church suffered from severe institutional problems, the period between the 1370s and the coming of Henry VIII's Reformation in the 1530s was one of flourishing of medieval religion at the ground level, within local communities and among individuals.

It was a period remarkable for building of parish churches and family chantries. It was a period in which cults of particular saints proliferated and visitation of their shrines flourished. In all towns and the larger villages, processions in which religious statues, pictures, and relics were carried through the streets took place very frequently.

Above all, the late fourteenth century was a period of flowering of English mysticism. Individuals who withdrew to caves or the tops of hills to meditate on union with God were much admired. The English mystical movement encompassed both kinds of mystical experience, the positive and the negative.

Positive mysticism was the traditional Platonic kind going back to the second century A.D., in which the saint disciplines himself or herself to reach up to God. Negative mysticism (more common in East Asia and fashionable in the United States today) involves the effort to cast off all consciousness of the body and individual personality, the creation of total material and intellectual emptiness, so that the torrent of divinity can rush in. It represents the sensibility closest to that of the seeker of nirvana to appear in European religious literature. The classic text of negative mysticism, *The Cloud of Unknowing,* was written anonymously by an English monk in Gaunt's lifetime. It merits a long extract:

> So for the love of God be careful and don't put any great strain on your mind or imagination. For I tell you truthfully, you cannot achieve it by any such strain, so leave your intellectual and your imaginative skills strictly alone.
>
> And don't imagine that because I refer to a "cloud" or "darkness" that I am talking about a cloud of vapours that evaporates into thin air or a darkness you see in your house when your candle has been extinguished. That is the kind of darkness you can imagine with some

degree of mental ingenuity on the brightest summer's day, just as on the darkest winter's night you can imagine a bright shining light. Do not you waste your time with any of these false ideas. I didn't mean anything like that. When I use the word "darkness" I mean an absence of knowledge, as when you say that the things you don't know or have forgotten are "dark" to you because you cannot see them with your inner eye. And for the same reason, this "cloud" is no cloud in the sky but a "cloud of unknowing" between you and your God . . .

If you want to stand fast in virtue and not fall prey to temptation, never let your intention fail. Beat constantly against the cloud of unknowing between you and your God with a piercing dart of longing love and be loath to let your mind wander on anything less than God. Don't give up for anything, because this is absolutely the only work that destroys the ground and root of sin. It doesn't matter how much you fast or keep long vigils, how early you get up, how hard your bed is or how painful your hair-shirt. Indeed, if it was lawful for you—as, of course, it isn't—to pluck out your eyes, cut your tongue from your mouth, stop your ears and nose, lop off your limbs and inflict all the pain that is possible or that you can imagine on your body, none of this would do you any good at all. The impulse and the temptation to sin would still be embedded in you.

What else can I tell you? However much you weep with remorse for your sins or sorrow for Christ's Passion or however firmly you fix your mind on the joys of heaven, what benefit would you derive? Certainly it would give you much good, much help, much profit, much grace. But compared with this blind yearning of love, it can do very little . . . For if this loving impulse is properly rooted in the soul, it contains all the virtues, truly, perfectly and effectually, without in any way diluting the intention of the will towards God. Indeed, it doesn't matter how many virtues a man acquires, without this true love they are bound to be warped and thus imperfect.

This is because virtue is nothing else but a properly ordered and deliberate turning of the soul to God. Why? God as he is in himself is the one and only source of all the virtues, so much so that if anyone is inspired to acquire a single virtue with mixed motives, even if God is uppermost in his mind, that virtue is bound to be flawed. We shall understand this better if we concentrate on just one or two particular virtues, and these may as well be humility and love. For anyone who has acquired these two virtues doesn't need any more; he has got them all.

Set to work, therefore, with all possible speed: beat against this high cloud of unknowing—you can rest later! It is extremely hard work for the beginner, make no mistake about that, unless God makes it easier with a special grace or simply because after a while one gets used to it.

But in what sense exactly is it hard work? Certainly not in the devout and urgent motion of love that is always springing up in the will of a contemplative, because this is not produced mechanically but by the hand of almighty God, who is always ready to act in each eager soul who has done and continues to do everything in his power to prepare himself for this work.

So why is it so arduous? Obviously in the trampling on all memory of God's creatures and keeping them enveloped by that cloud of forgetting I mentioned earlier. This really is hard work because *we* have to do it, with God's help; the other aspect of the work, which I have just described—the urgent impulse of love—is entirely the work of God. So do your part and, I promise you, that he will not fail to do his.

Get to work as soon as possible, then. Let me see how you are bearing up. Can't you see that God is waiting for you? For shame! After just a short, hard period of effort you will find the immense difficulty of the work beginning to ease. It is true that it is hard and repressive at the start, when your devotion is weak, but later when you are more devout what once seemed extremely arduous has become much easier and you can begin to relax. You may only have to make a little effort—or even no effort at all, because sometimes God does everything himself. But this doesn't always happen and never for very long but whenever he chooses and as he chooses. But you will be more than happy then, so let him do what he likes.

Now you are going to ask me how you can destroy this stark awareness of yourself. You might be thinking that if you destroy this sense of yourself, you will destroy everything else too and you will be right. But I will answer this fear by telling you that without a very special grace from God and without a particular aptitude on your part, you will never be able to get rid of this naked sense of self. For your part, this aptitude consists in a robust and profound sorrow of spirit.

But it is essential that you exercise discretion in this matter. You mustn't put any excessive strain on your body or soul but should, as it were, sit quietly, almost as if you were asleep and entirely saturated and immersed in sorrow. This is what true and complete sorrow is like and if you can achieve it you will find that it helps you. Everybody has a special reason for grief, but the person who has a deep experience of himself existing far apart from God feels the most acute sorrow. Any other grief seems trivial in comparison. Indeed, anybody who has never experienced this grief should be really sorry for himself because he has never felt perfect sorrow! Once we have acquired this sorrow it not only purifies our souls, but it takes away all the pain merited by sin and thus makes the soul capable of receiving that joy which takes from a man all sense of his own being . . .

Everybody should know and experience this sorrowful weariness with self in some way or other. God promises to teach his spiritual disciples according to his good pleasure, but there must be a corresponding readiness in the disciple's own soul and body as he ascends the ladder of contemplation and cultivates the right disposition before he can be wholly united to God in perfect love—or as perfectly as possible in this world—if God wills.

Translated by Karen Armstrong in The English Mystics, *published by kind permission of the author and Kyle Cathie Limited.*

The author of *The Cloud of Unknowing* was very possibly a Carmelite friar. This religious text fits in with the Carmelites' worldview.

The Carmelites were the later Gaunt's favorite religious order. In reading *The Cloud of Unknowing* we get a sense of the religious ambience in which Gaunt was immersed. It is a long way from the warrior ethos he shared with the Black Prince. There is no evidence that Gaunt tried to reach a Carmelite nirvana. But being subjected to this kind of extreme mysticism, as he was because of his attendance on the Carmelites, affected his sensibility. It helps to explain a certain diffidence and hesitancy in his behavior. We are all part of what we have met. Listening to mystical sermons of this kind must have had some effect on Gaunt's outlook in his later years.

The late fourteenth century was a time of brooding religious sensibility in England. A hundred years later, much of this radical sensibility was submerged by the advancement of classical humanism. But for now it was deeply expressed in religious literature.

The Cloud of Unknowing was at the Carmelite extreme on this band of sensibility. More moderate was the elegiac poem *Pearl*, written anonymously in the 1370s by a member of the gentry about one hundred miles north of Oxford. A recently deceased young girl is presented metaphorically as Pearl, to whom the grieving poet wants to communicate across the river of mortality but cannot, because he is held back by the inevitable corruption of his human nature:

> *Had I but sought to content my Lord*
> *And taken his gifts without regret,*
> *And held my place and heeded the word*
> *Of the noble Pearl so strangely met,*
> *Drawn heavenward by divine accord*
> *I had seen and heard more mysteries yet;*
> *But always men would have and hoard*
> *and gain the more, the more they get.*
> *So banished I was, by cares beset,*

From realms eternal untimely sent;

How madly, Lord, they strive and fret

Whose acts accord not with your content!

Translated by Marie Boroff in Pearl: A New Verse Translation,
by permission of W. W. Norton and Company. Copyright 1977
by W. W. Norton and Company.

This was common sentiment, as common as the chivalric and Arthurian literature recited in the great aristocratic dining halls. It was central to Gaunt's cultural ambience and it affected his mind-set and behavior. This was still a Christian world.

⌘

We are today two historical stages removed from medieval Christianity. The first stage was the Protestant and Catholic Reformations of the sixteenth century. The second stage, more revolutionary, was the steady rise of secularism during the nineteenth and twentieth centuries among industrialized and urbanized peoples.

The first stage was marked by efforts to return to earlier phases of Christianity and to impose more discipline upon both clergy and laity. The second stage was marked by withdrawal from church attendance and the decisive lessening—almost to the point of zero among some groups—of religious impact in daily life. Shaped by the two stages, we do not find it easy to uncover and realistically formulate the structure of medieval Christianity.

In the early years of the first century A.D., Christianity was a small sect in the radical fringe of Judaism. By A.D. 200 the Christian Church had separated itself from Judaism and had become the religion of a small but significant proportion of the population of the Roman empire. By A.D. 400 Christianity was the religion of 95 percent of the population of the Roman Empire. It was greatly aided by state authorization and by material and institutional support from the state.

In the course of this triumph Christianity itself underwent fundamental changes. Its emphasis hitherto on community, friendship, and spiritual equality was now restricted to the monastic orders. Instead, the Church emphasized the power to open the gates of Heaven and it was organized in a hierarchical form. One gained greater religious power, material well-being, and political influence the higher one ascended in this hierarchy, which culminated with the Bishop of Rome in the Latin West and the bishops of Constantinople, Alexandria, and Antioch in the Greek-speaking East.

The original sectarian, communal, personally friendly Church of the early first century A.D. was compromised into the hierarchical Church of the Middle Ages in three stages. First, ecclesiastical officials in the large cities of the Roman empire were almost inevitably bound to develop positions of leadership and greater wealth compared to the laity and the other, less fortunate clergy. Second, the authorization and support of the Church by the Roman state in the fourth century had a conservatizing and hierarchical effect on Church organization and teaching. But the third stage, the one with the most compromising impact on the Church, especially in the Latin West, came about through the enmeshing of the lay nobility with the Church after A.D. 800.

The compromising of the early Church by the medieval aristocracy took two forms. First, the Church taught a very conservative political doctrine of subservience to kings and lords: "The powers that be are ordained of God." Second, the aristocracy came to control the Church at various levels by providing "livings," sustainable income for the parish priests, and endowments for the monasteries, and had the right to interfere in the election of abbots of the larger monasteries plus a very substantial part in the appointment of clerics at the level of bishop and cathedral canon.

By 1050 ecclesiastics were talking about the intermixing of *ecclesia* and *mundus,* of church and world. The whole institutional structure and material foundations of the Latin Church were now dependent on the goodwill, generosity, and political action of the aristocracy. Compare this to the words of Jesus of Nazareth: "My kingdom is not of this world."

Knowledge of Church history was very meager in the Middle Ages. Ecclesiastical history began to be seriously pursued—first among Protestants—only in the sixteenth century. Except for the radical wing of the Franciscan order and a small group of heretics, the unquestionable true picture of the earliest Apostolic Church as emerging among the poor and humble was ignored.

Or it was explained away by saying that under Divine Providence, the Church and its senior personnel had, by God's will on the way to the Last Judgment, become rich and politically influential. In other words, the Church had reached its level of hierarchy, power, and wealth by historical evolution controlled by Christ. But even this historicizing doctrine was not sufficient for the papacy. It rejected the Spiritual Franciscans' doctrine of apostolic poverty and caused the radical wing of the Franciscan order to be disbanded.

In monasteries, nunneries, priories, and, much more rarely, among cathedral clergy, there was still an echo of the earliest Church—an egalitarian, friendly community of faithful. But even the "regular" (monastic) clergy had been subject to the impress of hierarchy. By the thirteenth century abbots no longer slept in communal dormitories and took their meals with the brethren. They lived in separate, upscale houses on the abbey's grounds and dined separately, often entertaining the aristocracy, of which—half the time, at least—they were offspring.

It is all the more remarkable, therefore, that Gaunt in his later years should have had a special affection for the Carmelite friars, a small religious order that, after the downfall of the radical Franciscans, most clearly echoed the communal, self-abnegating, impoverished original Church.

There was something in Gaunt's makeup that attracted him to these Carmelite exemplars of earliest Christianity.

The same subterranean character disposition played some part in attracting Gaunt to John Wyclif for a while. But while Gaunt in time came to be troubled by the radical implications of Wyclif's words and actions, he did not see the Carmelites' code as an implied criticism of the established Church. The Carmelites were part of a complex tapestry of ecclesiastical life. They were engaged in personal renewal, not reversion to Christianity to its original form, although no doubt they were inspired in part by the Church of poverty and friendship portrayed in the Gospels and the Book of Acts.

Most of the time, however, Gaunt, like the other aristocrats, accepted the Church that was highly visible—the hierarchical, wealthy, complex institution that was responsible for a distinctive culture and social organization we call medieval Christianity.

For Gaunt the Church was a congeries of ideas, practices, personnel, and artistic and literary forms that were central to the environment he lived in, part of the air he breathed. Just so do we accept Wall Street brokers and Harvard professors, in spite of their corruptions and limitations and defects, as overwhelmingly admirable groups to which we would be happy to belong. Gaunt readily accepted the teachings of the Church of his day. He could not conceive of the Church, in spite of its problems, as being other than highly beneficial to himself, his family, and society in general. The ecclesiastics were a bit disorganized and sometimes lacking in discipline—he saw that. But they were still on the whole worthy of respect and patronage.

There are some parts of the United States and Western Europe where this is still the prevailing view held of the Catholic Church today.

⬥⬥⬥

No one can appreciate the texture of medieval Christianity who has not seen and heard a candlelight procession of black-gowned nine- and ten-year-old boys in the nave of a cathedral.

No one can appreciate medieval Christianity who has not seen working people dressed in their Sunday best silently receiving the wafer and wine in communion at the altar.

No one can appreciate medieval Christianity who has not turned the parchment pages of an illuminated codex of a saint's life.

No one can appreciate medieval Christianity who has not run his eye and hand over the sculptured effigies of a lord and lady behind the altar of a church, as with Gaunt and Blanche at St. Paul's Cathedral in London.

Medieval Christianity was not going anywhere. It had no progressive vision other than the Last Judgment, which waited upon the Second Coming of Christ to the whole world, including the feared Muslims to the south and the inscrutable heathen Slavs to the East.

Until these ultimate events, the Church was in a condition of stasis, of waiting and stability, of application of all arts to the glory of God.

The great majority of people never saw their forty-fifth birthday, or even hoped to. The Church provided for nearly all of them the only high satisfactions they knew, including faith healing and the probability, after a suitable time paying for their sins in Purgatory, of heavenly reward.

The Church's vision closely resembled that of aristocrats like Gaunt. Cultivate in this short life what God has given you, and appreciate the divine message communicated through music and the visual arts—that, along with food, sex, and defecation. It was a still, wistful world but it was not without joy, faith, and love.

CHAPTER EIGHT

Peasants

IN JOHN OF GAUNT'S lifetime, 60 percent of the population of England were still peasants, that is, agricultural and pastoral workers and their families. Among these peasant families there was a vast variety in legal and economic status. Perhaps 60 percent of the peasants were freemen, or at least claimed to be. The other 40 percent were serfs, unfree peasants bound to the land, although serfdom had been on the decline since the mid-thirteenth century. Before Gaunt's time, there had never been anything resembling a revolt. Unfortunately for him, the calamitous fourteenth century would witness the first, and he would be a target.

The lords had not always wanted to keep peasants in a condition of serfdom. Serfdom had its own expenses for lords. By 1300, because of the population explosion of the previous hundred years, some lords figured it was cheaper to manumit the serfs, clear them from their ancestral village and strips of land that were legally their own, and turn the whole village into the lord's private domain worked by cheap day laborers.

Nothing distressed a landlord more than seeing an old, bent serf holding on to his strips of land along with garden plots and rights to public grazing land, while the old serf's level of productivity on the lord's land declined.

Lack of clarity as to the legal status of many peasants arose partly from failure on the part of some gentry and many peasants to keep documents of manumission. Even greater confusion arose from a loophole in the common law by which anyone who participated in any royal civil court action was deemed a freeman in the eyes of the law. Copies of the court records showing peasants litigating in the royal courts were expensive and not easy to come by. The legal status of a quarter of the peasantry was therefore under dispute.

⌇⌇⌇

Before the Norman Conquest of 1066, the English peasants were freemen living in self-governing village communities. The conquest of England by William the Conqueror and a thousand French soldiers changed all that. The English peasantry was forced down into serfdom, which meant that a peasant family was bound to the land they were cultivating. In that way the French lord was always assured of a labor supply. If your father was a serf, so were you.

When William the Conqueror replaced the English bishops and the abbots of the major monasteries with Frenchmen recruited from all over the northern half of France, the legal status of the serfs was frozen in place. The bishops and abbots, who were lords of the great ecclesiastical estates, kept careful records. They showed the lay nobility that operating a system of French serfdom effectively in England required the careful keeping of records to assure that serf status in a peasant family was perpetuated indefinitely.

When the Cistercian order of monks developed their great sheep and cattle ranges in northern England in the mid-twelfth century, these "white monks" (as they were called from their habits) also enserfed the workers on the ranges. The village communities lost their self-government. A steward of the lord now presided over the village courts, and his word was law.

What severely weakened serfdom in the thirteenth century was the extension of royal law, the common law, over the country. The royal justices sought to create a national system of law. In so doing they reduced the village courts' jurisdiction to dealing with misdemeanors and petty land disputes, and transferred felonies and important civil action to the royal, common-law courts.

Serfdom was not easily compatible with this ambitious nationalization of the common law presided over by panels of royal judges in the county courts. "King's Law" replaced "folk law." The common law worked like a giant vacuum cleaner, drawing the peasants out of the lord's village courts and thereby giving many peasant families their freedom between 1250 and 1450. The lords resisted, but by Gaunt's time three-quarters of the peasantry had gained freedom. By 1380 the village courts had lost their power over rural life. They remained as empty judicial shells.

The county courts were steadily becoming the venue for peasants as well as gentry, elevating the peasants' judicial status to that of freemen. With so many litigants in the county courts, the royal government had to create the office of justice of the peace, by which four times a year, in their quarter sessions, panels of wealthy gentry dealt with misdemeanors, giving the royal justices in the county court more time to deal with felonies (hanging offenses) and substantial lawsuits about ownership of land. This remained the main structure of the English legal system until the late nineteenth century.

༄

Just as the peasants varied in legal status, they varied in wealth. There were entrepreneurial peasant families that bought up land for their progeny. This became a more visible trend when the peasant population in the fourteenth century declined markedly due to famine and disease. Real estate prices declined; peasant families died out and the wealthy peasants—called yeomen in the fifteenth century—could strike deals to get hold of vacant land. On the other hand, a quarter of the peasants were landless cotters, or day laborers, who lived perpetually on the edge of unemployment and starvation.

The desperate condition of the poor and landless peasantry is graphically described in *Piers Plowman,* a long,
meandering religious poem written during Gaunt's lifetime.
Its author called himself William Langland. He is believed to
have been a London priest who had previously served in a
country parish.

Langland gives us a picture of various classes in peasant
society. Even among the more secure and landed peasants
there is a constant struggle to fill stomachs. The cottagers, or
landless peasants, live a life of boundless misery:

> *The most needy are our neighbours, if we notice right well,*
> *As prisoners in pits and poor folk in cottages,*
> *Charged with their children, and chief lord's rent,*
> *What by spinning they save, they spend it in house-hire,*
> *Both in milk and in meal to make a mess of porridge,*
> *To cheer up their children who chafe for their food,*
> *And they themselves suffer surely much hunger*
> *And woe in the winter, with waking at nights*
> *And rising to rock an oft restless cradle,*
> *Both to card and to comb, to clout and to wash,*
> *To rub and to reel yarn, rushes to peel,*
> *So 'tis pity to proclaim or in poetry to show*
> *The woe of these women who work in such cottages;*
> *And of many other men who much woe suffer,*
> *Crippled with hunger and with thirst, they keep up appearances,*
> *And are abashed for to beg, and will not be blazoned*

What they need from their neighbours, at noon and at evensong.
This I know full well, for the world has taught me,
How churls are afflicted who have many children,
And have no coin but their craft to clothe and to keep them,
And full many to feed and few pence to do it.
With bread and penny-ale that is less than a pittance,
Cold flesh and cold fish, instead of roast venison;
And on Fridays and feast days a farthing's worth of mussels
Would be a feast for such folk, or else a few cockles.
'Twere a charity to help those that bear such charges,
And comfort such cottagers, the crippled and blind.

Translated by Terence Tiller in The Vision of Piers Plowman,
by permission of BBC Enterprise Limited

Langland was a proto-Malthusian. The excessive number of children among the landless peasants contributed to their dire poverty, he stressed. Contraception was not unknown in the Middle Ages; condoms were made out of goatskin. But the poor peasants never heard of mechanical contraception. Its use was rare. Gaunt never used a condom, but he could well afford to have a lot of children.

It was possible to be a free peasant and be poor and to be a serf and be prosperous, but generally speaking, growing wealth was associated with a baseline of legal freedom. That was the view of the peasants themselves.

In the thirty years after the Black Death, there was a rise in class consciousness among the peasantry and the emergence of some semblance of activism among the populace in some parts of rural England, especially toward the east and south. There were several causes for this emergence of peasant class identity.

Growing literacy, mainly in English, among the peasants, due to a proliferation of village elementary schools, produced radical consequences. Itinerant radical Franciscan friars, as well as Lollards such as John Ball, harangued the village populace in English about their grievances and projected a vision of a more just society organized along Christian lines. In addition, the French and Spanish navies conducted guerrilla runs on the south coast of England and there was justifiable resentment among the peasants that the great lords and the royal government did not put a stop to these depredations.

After the Black Death, when supply and demand began to push up the cost of rural labor, Parliament, at the behest of landlords, set a ceiling on wage rates by legislation. In order to raise money for prospective fighting in France, the government also imposed for the first time a poll (head) tax that was onerous and hard to evade. Finally, as a by-product of the infighting among the grand dukes to gain control over the royal council, a general slovenliness prevailed in administration and law, allowing for subversive organization among the peasants.

In June of 1381 peasant rioting broke out in East Anglia and Kent, guided by the peasants' own class leaders, the Lollard preacher John Ball and a certain Wat Tyler. The rebels began to seize and burn legal and tax records. They then attacked members of the establishment whom they could lay their hands on, including the Archbishop of Canterbury, Simon of Sudbury, whom they caught in the countryside and killed. They exhibited discipline and planning by marching on London, and many thousands occupied a field in the London suburbs, where they demanded to see the young King Richard II, whom they naively believed was on their side.

The royal officials cowered for protection in the Tower of London, but Richard II, then thirteen years old, put a crown on his head, mounted his white horse, and with only a small bodyguard went out to meet the rebels. Early on in the discussion, one of the King's bodyguards killed Wat Tyler. This was the crucial moment when a full-scale revolution could have occurred. But young Richard leaped into the breach and assured the rebels that justice would be done, that freedom would ring out, that he was on their side. If they would only go home, all would be well. It was a remarkable performance for a pubescent king.

The rebels did leave, but a handful crossed the Thames to the Strand. There they encountered the huge Savoy Palace. They burned it to the ground, first looting the fine furniture and emptying the wine cellar.

The Savoy Palace was John of Gaunt's London residence and was reputed to be the most impressive private house in the city. Its location on the Strand, on the banks of the Thames, made access to it easy at a time when the river was the prime highway through London. Here in the Savoy,

Gaunt hosted lords, gentry, and burgesses when Parliament was in session. Here the Duke showed off his artworks and rare jewels to other members of the royal family. Here he received petitions for largesse and support from a wide spectrum of people, including Oxford professors. Gaunt's other favorite residence was Pontefract Castle in the north, distant and too remote for most petitioners.

The greater part of Gaunt's estates were in the Duchy of Lancaster in the northwest of the country, far from the brunt of the peasants' rebellion. But he also had estates in the southern and eastern parts of the country, and there the devastation was severe. Manor rolls were burned by the rebels. For many years, rents could not be collected, nor could lower courts meet.

ᕗᴍᴍᕁ

The most detailed account of the Peasants' Revolt is to be found in the *Anonymous Chronicle* put together in a monastery in York, in northern England. Inserted in the *Chronicle* there is a detailed account of the revolt, probably written by a lower-level government official, perhaps a lawyer or tax collector, or possibly by a cathedral canon or even a merchant. The account is written in French. It reveals both the general ferocity of the uprising and personal animosity of "the commons" (the peasants) toward John of Gaunt and his officials.

At this time [1381] the commons of southern England
suddenly rose in two groups, one in Essex and the other

in Kent. They directed their evil actions against the duke of Lancaster and the other lords of the realm because of the exceptionally severe tenths and fifteenths [taxes] and other subsidies lightly conceded in parliaments and extortionately levied from the poor people. These subsidies did nothing for the profit of the kingdom but were spent badly and deceitfully to the great impoverishment of the commons . . . and it was for this reason . . . that the commons rose.

At this time the commons had as their counsellor a chaplain of evil disposition named Sir John Balle, who advised them to get rid of all the lords, archbishops, bishops, abbots and priors as well as most of the monks and canons so that there should be no bishop in England except for one archbishop, namely himself; no religious house should hold more than two monks or canons, and their possessions should be divided among the laity. For which advice he was regarded as a prophet by the commons, and laboured with them day by day to strengthen them in their malice. He was well rewarded later by being drawn, disembowelled, hanged and beheaded as a traitor.

After this the commons went to many towns and raised the people there, some willingly and some not, until a good sixty thousand were gathered together. On their journey towards London they met several men of law and twelve of the king's knights, whom they captured

and forced to swear that they would support the commons under threat of execution. They did much damage
in Kent, notably to Thomas de Heseldene, servant of the
duke of Lancaster, because of their hatred for the said
duke. They cast his manors and houses to the ground
and sold his live-stock—horses, oxen, cows, sheep and
pigs—and all sorts of corn [grain] at a cheap price. Every
day the commons were eager to have his head . . .

Sir Robert Bealknap, Chief Justice of the Common
Bench, was sent into the country on a commission of
trailbaston [criminal proceeding against gangsterism].
Indictments against various persons were laid before
him, and the people of the area were so fearful that they
proposed to abandon their holdings. Wherefore the
commons rose against him and came before him to tell
him that he was a traitor to the king and kingdom and
was maliciously proposing to undo them by the use of
false inquests taken before him. Accordingly they made
him swear on the Bible that never again would he hold
such sessions nor act as a justice in such inquests. And
they forced him to tell them the names of all the jurors.
They captured all of these jurors that they could,
beheaded them and threw their houses to the ground.
And Sir Robert travelled home as quickly as possible.
Afterwards, and before Whitsunday, fifty thousand of
the commons gathered, going to the various manors
and townships of those who would not rise with them,

throwing their buildings to the ground and setting them ablaze . . . They proposed to kill all the lawyers, jurors and royal servants they could find. Meanwhile all the great lords and other notable people of that country [Kent] fled towards London or to other counties where they might be safe.

Translated by C. Oman and R. B. Dobson in The Peasants'
Revolt of 1381, *edited by R. B. Dobson (New York:
St. Martin's Press, 1970)*

Why did the peasants hate John of Gaunt so much? There are three reasons. First, he stood out at the head of the aristocratic class. He was of royal blood and owned estates and houses all over the kingdom. He had the largest and most beautiful house in London, in a prominent location on the Strand where its presence in the city loomed large.

Gaunt entertained lavishly. He rode along the roads bypassing peasant homes with a large bodyguard of horsed soldiers, their armor shining and clacking. It was impossible, even for many peasants, not to be aware of Gaunt, and he symbolized the landlord class that the peasants of 1381 felt oppressed them. They wanted a share of the wealth and comfort that Gaunt so obviously possessed.

Second, Gaunt was a tough landlord. His peasants were constantly under the supervision and scrutiny of the dozens of stewards and fiscal managers the Duke employed. To maintain Gaunt's lifestyle and his commitments as a warrior, these functionaries kept records and presided over courts that squeezed every possible drop of revenue from the workers and their families.

Third, Gaunt suffered from exposure through the primitive, oral media of his day—the sermons and broadsides of radical spokesmen, like John Ball and Wat Tyler. Radical leaders always need an image of human evil they can raise up to excite the rabble. Gaunt, who never made a public statement against the Peasants' Revolt and played little or no role in punishing the rebels, was a convenient scapegoat in the conflicts of the times.

Gaunt was not in London in harm's way when angry peasants burned down the Savoy Palace. But the incident deeply affected him. It caused him to see himself less as a Londoner, more as a northerner. He made no attempt to rebuild the Savoy, nor did he build for himself a new town house. Instead, Gaunt rented a house in the suburbs from a rich ecclesiastic whenever he needed accommodations in London for an extended period, as during a meeting of Parliament.

Gaunt realized that he had become a symbol of the unjust old order for the restless lower classes. He had become an object of hatred and fear in the villages and streets. Recognition of his unpopularity drove him to seek authorization and fiscal support from King and Parliament for his effort to gain the Castilian throne, which would take him out of England. Five years later, in 1386, he departed for his ill-fated campaign in Spain.

King Richard's promise of freedom and justice for the peasants was not fulfilled. Not even amnesty was granted. Instead, the royal government authorized special panels of judges to try the leaders of the Peasant Revolt and hang them. This was the fate of the Lollard preacher and revolutionary leader John Ball.

The anger and hatred of the peasants and their admiration for the Lollard preacher, however, lay deep in society:

Pleas [trials in the county court] held, on Thursday 16 July 1381, before Hugh la Zouche and his fellows, assigned to hear, punish and chastise the rebels and disturbers of the peace in the said county [of Cambridge].

John Shirle of the county of Nottingham was taken because it was found that he had been a vagabond [*vagabundus*] in various counties during the whole time of the disturbance, insurrection and tumult, carrying lies as well as silly and worthless talk from district to district, whereby the peace of the lord the king could rapidly be broken and the people be disquieted and disturbed. Among other damaging words, namely after the proclamation of the peace of the lord the king made on the aforesaid day and year, when the justices assigned by the lord the king were holding sessions in the town, he said in a tavern in Briggestrete [Bridge Street] in Cambridge, where many were assembled to listen to his news and worthless talk, that the stewards of the lord

the king as well as the justices and many other officers
and ministers of the king were more deserving to be
drawn and hanged and to suffer other lawful pains and
torments than John Balle, chaplain, a traitor and felon
lawfully convicted. For John Shirle said that he [Ball]
had been condemned to death falsely, unjustly and for
envy by the same ministers with the king's assent,
because he was a true and worthy man, prophesying
things useful to the commons of the kingdom and
telling of wrongs and oppressions done to the people by
the king and the aforesaid ministers; and Ball's death
would not go unpunished but within a short space of
time he would well reward both the king and his said
ministers and officers. These sayings and threats
redound to the prejudice of the crown of the lord the
king and to the contempt and manifest disturbance of
the people. And thereupon the said John Shirle was
immediately brought by the sheriff before the said justices sitting at Cambridge castle; and he was charged
about these matters and was diligently examined as
regards his conversation, his presence [in Cambridge]
and his estate; and when these things had been
acknowledged by him before the said justices, his evil
behaviour and condition were made plainly manifest
and clear. And thereupon trustworthy witnesses in his
presence at the time when the abovementioned lies, evil
words, threats and worthless talk had been spoken by

him, were requested; and they, being sworn to speak the truth about these matters, testified that all the aforesaid words imputed to him had indeed been spoken by him; and he, examined once again, did not deny the charges laid against him. Therefore by the discretion of the said justices he was hanged.

Edited and translated by R. B. Dobson in The Peasants' Revolt of 1381

Gaunt did not participate actively in the royal government's repression of the peasants. Nor did he oppose it. Gaunt was aware that the rebellious peasants had singled him out as a prime enemy. It was best to keep a low profile in this class war.

In the first half of the fifteenth century there were aftershocks to the explosion of 1381. The Lollard insurrection in 1414 led by Sir John Oldcastle had some class and ideological implications. In 1450 there was a localized rebellion in Kent led by an obscure member of the lower gentry, Jack Cade.

The tectonic plates of the old rural society were moving. Serfdom was disappearing and along with it an economy of low yield and little change, to be replaced by the beginnings of rural capitalism. It was not the preachers and their visionary dreams of an egalitarian Christian society that would prevail. It was the market-minded gentry and the yeomen with their building up of estates worked by insecure day laborers that were benefiting by the impact of capitalism on the old rural society that had been in place since the eleventh century.

Gaunt's capable estate managers must have made him aware of some of this transformation in rural society. For the Duke this meant only more keen attention to the micro and macro movements of the land market. As with today's billionaires, the context of social change meant for Gaunt the need for more careful management and identification of opportunities. Peasant outrage and Christian idealism were at best novel environmental conditions that had to be considered and whose consequences had to be avoided.

〇‍‍‍〇

There would be no working-class movement again in England until the early 1650s, as an aftermath of the English Civil Wars and temporary displacement of the monarchy by a Protestant military dictatorship under Oliver Cromwell. A group called the Diggers set about digging up the common land in a handful of villages, expropriating the land for the working class and the poor. Another group, the Fifth Monarchy Men, envisioned a messianic socialist republic. The military dictatorship easily suppressed these pockets of radical working-class activism.

Not until the founding of the Labour Party in the last decade of the nineteenth century was there again an organized working-class movement in England. The Labour government of 1945–1951 tried to establish a welfare state in England, offering protection and benefits to the working class. Vestiges of this attempt to create a socialist commonwealth in England still endure, particularly the National Health Service. But in the late 1990s, under another Labour government, there was a massive withdrawal from socialism and an enfeeblement of working-class solidarity.

In the end, the billionaires have triumphed, as they did in 1381. Gaunt would feel at home in today's London. He would find that the name of his palace on the Strand, the Savoy, has been taken up by one of London's most exclusive hotels. He would reserve a palatial suite of rooms for himself at the Savoy hotel and give fancy dinner parties. The tabloid press would idolize Gaunt and the royal family give him due deference. Undoubtedly, Oxford would award him an honorary degree.

The important point is not that perhaps a third of the peasantry exploded in rebellion in 1381, but how well members of the ruling class like Gaunt learned their lesson. The poll tax was never collected. The government abandoned trying to set a ceiling on wages.

Gaunt and the aristocracy took a moderate and far-seeing approach to the condition of the peasantry. The market was allowed to function with a high degree of autonomy. The market was allowed to set wages, and by the time of Gaunt's death in 1399, the market was achieving stability. The great demand for peasant labor and escalation of rural workers' wages that had followed the Black Death of 1348 and 1361 now abated. The peasants were left to contend with the invisible hand of the market.

The Peasants' Revolt of 1381 taught the ruling class a lesson. There was no need to use parliamentary legislation to repress the rural working class. The market would do the job.

In the sixteenth century the English peasantry suffered from the enclosure movement. A quarter of the peasantry were driven off their small holdings, which were now enclosed by hedges to protect capitalist agricultural innovations.

This drastic change, however, was accomplished not through parliamentary legislation but through the common-law courts, sustaining the market economy, as they do today. Once the rural market economy got going in Gaunt's time, along with eliminating what was left of serfdom, it swept away the vestiges of the early medieval peasant community. Gaunt and the landlords learned from the Peasants' Revolt that it was risky to use legislation to hurry this capitalist revolution along. It would occur anyway by action of the market, helped by King's Law.

CHAPTER NINE

Politics

LIKE ANY PROMINENT billionaire and property owner today, Gaunt, Duke of Lancaster, was involved in two kinds of politics, local and national. The local politics consisted of Gaunt's relationship with the landowners, from the highest ranks of the gentry down to the yeomen, the free and wealthier peasants. They resided in the counties, mainly in the north of the country, where the Duke held vast estates and where his influence in local government and law was strong.

Some of the wealthier families among the gentry were bound to the Duke of Lancaster by contractual arrangements that had originated decades earlier. But these old feudal contracts in the form of elaborate, ornate documents called charters had to be periodically reviewed and sometimes rewritten to mutual advantage. Arrangements with some of the upper gentry, the lower gentry, towns, and the top stratum of the yeomen were of recent and such ever-changing character that, judging from the thousands of documents issued in Gaunt's name, whether from the Savoy Palace in London or a castle in the north, this business was the constant activity of the clerks in the Duke's chancery, or writing office.

Copies of these documents were retained in the Duke's chancery and from time to time were pasted end to end in fat rolls, called registers.

The documents are mostly written in French because they were addressed to lords, gentry, and merchants whose Latin was weak or nonexistent; some, addressed to churchmen, are in Latin. More than half the items included are the short documents called indentures. These are contractual agreements drawn up by the Duke's administration acting on his behalf and sealed with his personal seal. The documents are written with a pen or stylus on parchment. Messengers were busy on the roads, carrying the indentures and letters to their addressees and the responses back to the Duke.

In an indenture, the Duke promises to do something to help the other (socially inferior) party to the agreement— give that party's family more land, allow hunting on the Duke's estate, reduce rent, bestow a pension, provide a local government office, or support him in an important lawsuit. The indenture also specifies the obligations of the nonducal recipient: to pay rent, provide service of one kind or another, give the Duke wood or meat or produce once or twice a year, or attend to administrative matters on or near the Duke's estate.

When armies were raised to fight in France or Spain, the flow of indentures from the Duke's document office increased at a feverish pace, because this was how armies were organized and paid. The Duke would pay a stipend, or a pension for so many years of military service, and would compensate the other party to the indenture, a captain, for raising a defined number of equipped and armed soldiers. The soldiers were to congregate at a certain place on a given day, usually one of the southern ports—Portsmouth was a favorite—in four to eight weeks.

In return, the Duke's administrators were supposed to recover the costs outlined in the military indenture from the royal treasury, with the funds coming ultimately from a tax approved by Parliament. All the people accompanying the Duke abroad were thus mercenaries, except very rarely for a handful of aristocrats and wealthy gentry who served out of loyalty to and intimacy with the Duke.

The royal government was always in arrears, sometimes for several years, in compensating Gaunt for his outlay to his captains and ordinary mercenaries. He had to pay at least half the cost of his Spanish expedition out of his own pocket. At his death, after a long career as a general, Gaunt was probably still in the red with regard to military expenses.

Gaunt, with his administrators, had to keep the indentured soldiers contented because, when they were not at war, they were many of the same people he had to deal with in matters of lands, rents, local administrative services, peace-keeping in the countryside, and the functioning of the law courts in the counties he dominated. He was not always able to keep them happy, since the royal government so often fell behind in reimbursing him.

In the early stages of the Hundred Years' War, even common mercenaries could pick up cash on the side from looting French estates, towns, and farms, or holding for ransom French knights they captured on the battlefield. When a truce was declared, the mercenaries went home with their loot or ransom money, bought land, and started or upgraded gentry or yeoman families. But after about 1370, as the war wound down, the chances for this rapacious behavior diminished.

The problem of local politics for Gaunt was therefore this: The thousands of indentured captains and soldiers he needed for regiments were also the people he had to deal with in the functioning of local economy and law. They were his constituents, and like all politicians, he had to keep his supporters happy. Sometimes it was too expensive to do this, and discontent in the countryside led to difficulty in collecting rents and taxes and keeping the peace.

The discontent could even mean that demobilized and angry mercenaries would form rural criminal gangs, loot peaceful farms, or audaciously invade the Duke's own estates and hunting grounds.

These gangs also provided for "maintenance" of their members in the county law courts through bribing and pressuring royal judges and suborning juries. Only one in seven of malefactors indicted by grand juries was ever convicted at trial, about the same proportion as in New York City today. The rest plea-bargained, were pardoned, or simply absconded into the forests like Robin Hood. Local politics, therefore, offered the Duke persistent problems and small agonies.

That some of the indentures, letters, and other documents in the Duke's Register deal with the same matters over and over again may indicate that Gaunt had taken a personal interest in the matters they dealt with. In spite of his high profile on the national and European scene, local politics and the contentedness of his constituents had to be important to him.

But that many of the petty issues mentioned in the Register—four volumes in small print, covering about 60 percent of the years of Gaunt's maturity, the registers for the other years having been lost—do not appear to have achieved resolution indicates that the Duke had only so much time and energy personally to devote to these local matters.

In the majority of instances he left it to his hardworking and sorely pressed officials and secretaries to face up to the local problems as best they could. After all, what Gaunt was most interested in with respect to the countryside and the streets was his income. If there were social tensions aplenty, and functioning of the law at the local level was falling prey to gangsterism, he could not deal obsessively with many such details.

Gaunt's involvement in national politics involved his relations with Parliament and his connection to his nephew

King Richard II. As a grand magnate and prominent member of the royal family, he had to get personally involved in these issues of national politics. They were not matters his clerks could handle by issuing documents.

⌘

The English Parliament was, in its beginning in the reign of Edward I in the late thirteenth century, an instrument of the king. Parliament was a special meeting of the king's Great Council of magnates, a group of lords and ecclesiastics ever ready to be summoned to Westminster and give the king advice. He often asked the magnates to approve going to war and the levying of special taxes to fight the war.

When, in addition to the summoned magnates, representatives of the larger towns ("the burgesses") and the gentry of the shire ("the knights") were summoned, the meeting was called a Parliament. By the mid-fourteenth century such a Parliament was summoned once or twice a year and was in session for about three weeks. In the early years of Parliament, representatives of the lower clergy (priests, friars, and professors) were also summoned, but this practice was suspended around 1330 because the voices of the lower clergy turned out to be sometimes dangerously radical, as was the case with some Franciscan friars.

The bishops and a very small group of abbots of large and old monasteries continued to be summoned to Parliament. The bishops and abbots also met with the lower clergy in their own assembly, called a convocation; such a body still meets.

Around 1340 the magnates (lords and ecclesiastics) and the representatives of the counties and towns (knights and burgesses) split apart into distinct corporate "houses," called the House of Lords and the House of Commons. The Lords met in the royal palace at Westminster. The Commons met in the chapter house (monks' meeting room) of Westminster Abbey.

The Lords were (and still are) summoned by the monarch by "private," or individual, writs of summons. That made someone officially a great lord. The Commons were summoned by common or collective writs: the king instructed the sheriff of the county to see to it that representatives of the gentry were elected and the mayors and aldermen were to choose urban representatives.

In Gaunt's lifetime the Commons were compensated for their expenses. By the sixteenth century this practice had ceased, and it was not resumed until 1911. The Lords paid their own way and would have been insulted if the king had offered to cover their expenses.

The burgesses representing the towns were chosen by the oligarchic town councils, the mayors and aldermen. In practice this meant that wealthy merchants represented the towns. The members of Parliament for the counties were nominally elected by the gentry who attended monthly meetings of the county court. In practice there could be open elections and the two MPs chosen were usually but not always from rich gentry families. The sheriff might choose, however, not to hold an actual election but simply consult with the leading gentry families as to who should be chosen.

Parliament in the time of Gaunt had three sorts of functions. In ascending order of importance these were propaganda, legal and judicial functions, and taxation. Propaganda meant that the king sat on his throne surrounded by his magnates and the Commons stood humbly in front of him. The king, or his chancellor on his behalf, made important announcements and invariably ended by asking for money and giving reasons why this taxation was urgent.

There were three aspects to the legal functions of Parliament. First, Lords could be tried for serious crimes, including treason. The House of Lords retained this function until 1925. Nominally it still does, and it is the highest court in England, but the actual presiding over trials is done by twenty-five professional lawyers. Second, MPs could petition the king for such things as pardons for well-connected criminals or repair of roads and bridges in specific localities.

By the 1350s a third legal function had been accorded Parliament: the passing of new laws, called statutes. But changes in the law came much more often from decisions in the royal courts than from parliamentary legislation.

Before the 1340s Parliament could and occasionally did meet without a grant of extraordinary taxation being requested. But from the mid-fourteenth century until the end of the great war with France in 1453, requests for money invariably were made. The Parliament gave the king a customs tax over exports (wool) and imports (wine). He needed approval of Parliament if he wanted to increase the customs rate—or at least so the MPs claimed.

The big infusion of money into the royal treasury, which made the intermittent war with France possible, was the grant of the "tenth and fifteenth" tax on the value of movable property (not land) and income. The knights and burgesses paid the tenth; the lords the lesser amount, the fifteenth. This inequity separated commoners from the more privileged aristocracy.

The king, the royal family, and the courtiers and members of the royal household looked upon Parliament and especially the Commons as mostly a necessary evil that could not be cast aside, because of the need for subsidies, as the parliamentary taxes came to be called. But until 1376 the royal government pretty well got what it wanted out of Parliament.

In that year, Parliament showed a surprising degree of independence; there occurred something that sounds like real political debate in Commons, and the procedures of Parliament were changed in two respects. The Commons now had a Speaker to preside over their sessions and represent them to the king, his councillors, and the Lords.

Commons was morphing under Gaunt's eyes from a special tax-approving council of the upper middle class into a deliberating legislative body. Instead of rubber-stamping new taxes on income and movable property, it wanted an accounting of how previously voted taxes had been spent. It had become a national legislature that debated the king's business.

Gaunt must have sensed that his great-grandfather Edward I had made a mistake in creating the national assembly of Parliament. French kings made no such error before 1789. They obtained approval of new taxes from isolated provincial assemblies, not a national legislature that a handful of outspoken gentry could mobilize against the royal government.

A judicial procedure was introduced, called impeachment, by which the Commons could indict the king's ministers for high crimes and misdemeanors. The Lords acted as a jury. If the indictments were sustained, removal from office, heavy fines, and imprisonment could be imposed on the alleged ministerial malefactors or in some instances bankers or merchants who trafficked in royal finances. (In 1787 an impeachment procedure was included in the newly formed Constitution of the United States.)

Because of these changes and the general politicization of Commons and its striving for a high degree of autonomy, the Parliament of 1376 came to be called the Good Parliament. The ultimate enemy that the Good Parliament aimed at was John of Gaunt. The royal officials and merchants who were impeached were members of his entourage. All this occurred while Edward III was slowly dying. Edward the Black Prince was already dead. The Black Prince's son,

Richard II, who would come to the throne in 1377, was not yet ten at the time. This left Gaunt to be the front man for the royal government and the object of parliamentary hostility. He stood out in front and referred to the Commons as "plebs," the lower class in Roman society, as he asked for a subsidy for the war.

Led by their Speaker, Sir Peter de la Mare, the Commons refused to proceed to vote a subsidy. Instead they impeached several government officials who were accused of corruption and mismanaging the war in France; a couple of merchants who were accused of making excess profits through fiscal relations with the Crown; and Alice Perrers, Edward III's mistress, on grounds of corruption

In general, the Commons, through their Speaker, complained that the King "has with him certain councillors and servants who were not loyal or profitable to him or the kingdom and they have made gains by subtlely, thus deceiving our lord the king." (Translated by G. Holmes.) The culprits were deemed to be Richard Lyons, a merchant, and William Latimer, a bureaucrat. Alice Perrers was accused of costing the king two thousand to three thousand pounds a year, an enormous sum.

Gaunt was at too high a level to be attacked directly by the Commons. A dozen people impeached by the Commons, however, were convicted by the Lords. There was nothing that Gaunt, for the moment, could do to outflank the Commons to save them.

The Good Parliament looks like the beginning of liberal democracy in England—the Commons versus the Crown. But actually it represented more the beginning of a split in the royal family that was to lead, in the mid-fifteenth century, to the Wars of the Roses, the civil war over the throne between two factions of the Plantagenet dynasty.

Sir Peter de la Mare, Speaker of the House of Commons, was the steward or chief estate manager of the Earl of March, who was married to a granddaughter of Edward III. The royal princes and great nobles who hated and feared Gaunt, and Gaunt's Lancastrian faction, congregated around the Earl of March, his royal wife, and their descendants. From this group was to emerge in the fifteenth century the Yorkists, the countervailing royal faction to the Lancastrians.

Gaunt showed by his retreat in the face of the Earl of March and the anti-Lancastrians in 1376 what a good politician he was. He could not withstand the oppositional Commons led by Sir Peter de la Mare; he could not save the impeached courtiers, bureaucrats, and merchant bankers, at least for the moment. Instead, Gaunt directed his attention to the next meeting of Parliament, in 1377. Because of pressure on the sheriffs, many of the oppositional MPs were not reelected. The newly elected Commons were easily manipulated by Gaunt and the Lancastrian party. Now it was Gaunt's steward who was chosen Speaker.

Nearly all the people impeached and convicted in the Good Parliament were let off by what came to be known as

the Merciless Parliament (mercilessly pro-Gaunt, that is) of
1377. Alice Perrers retired quietly to the estate given her by
Edward III. There was still much hostility to Gaunt, especially in the streets of London. He was suspected by courtiers
and London street people alike of wanting to supplant his
young nephew and make himself king.

Gaunt was an innovator in organizing elections to Commons. He saw that if Commons was no longer a passive tax-
voting council, that if it had become a political chamber with
a royalist group supporting Lancaster and the royal government, and an opposition group—"the country party," as they
came to be called in the sixteenth century—then attention
must be paid to how the MPs were chosen.

In the counties it was the sheriff who ran the election of
MPs at a meeting of the county court and made "return of
writs," that is, certified to the royal government the names
of the two MPs who were chosen. At least two-thirds of the
time there was no actual election process. The sheriff consulted with the leading gentry families and decided who
should be selected as MPs. This gave the sheriffs, who were
royal officials, a wide latitude in specifying who the MPs from
the counties would be. If an election had to be held because
there was vocal conflict among the gentry families, it was the
sheriff who counted the votes. He would go to a barn in the
county seat accompanied by thirty to seventy electors. He
would line up the supporters of two candidates along one wall
and the supporters of two other candidates along the facing

wall. (There was no secret ballot until the nineteenth century.) In a close vote the sheriff decided the election, since he did the counting. A brazen sheriff getting his marching orders from London would count only the side he favored.

The election of MPs from the towns was in the hands of each town's mayor and aldermen. They were easily persuaded or suborned by the royal government. A favorite threat was to rumble about cancellation of the royal charter by which the town exercised its internal autonomy and self-government.

It was Gaunt who started this system and put it into practice. It was still nakedly in operation in 1600. The amazing thing—and it tells us something about the gentry's independent temperament—is that some opposition candidates were nevertheless chosen.

⟨∭⟩

There is no evidence that Gaunt made any effort to replace Richard II. A few months after Gaunt's death, in 1399, the throne was taken from Richard by Gaunt's son Henry Bolingbroke, who became Henry IV. But this was something Gaunt had not foreseen or planned. He had done everything possible to prop up his erratic nephew.

Richard was ten years old when his grandfather Edward III died in 1377. Richard had been brought up in a negligent manner in the royal court. His mother, Joan of Kent, Princess of Wales, was absent most of the time, pursuing private and courtly matters. Richard was indulged by the courtiers. With the presence of Alice Perrers, the court was an oversexed, corrupt place and not suitable for raising a child. Nevertheless Richard II was relatively well educated. He was highly literate and was a musician. He was also undisciplined, selfish, overindulgent, and lazy.

As a young king Richard gathered around him a group of wild young men from the nobility much like himself. He formed a homosexual attachment to Robert de Vere, Earl of Oxford, upon whom he lavished gifts and much attention. Thereby Richard aroused the hostility of some of the leading magnates, including his uncle the Duke of Gloucester. These formed the Lords Appellant of 1386–1387, who removed the king's household officials and exiled de Vere.

Richard bided his time and with the help of John of Gaunt stabilized his government in the 1390s. He was probably the richest king in Europe. With Gaunt's acquiescence, he turned against the Lords Appellant, led by the Duke of Gloucester, in 1398 and had them murdered, sometimes with legal cover, sometimes by assassination.

Richard's paranoid seeking for revenge because of his lost lover and what he thought of as his mistreatment by the Lords Appellant frightened two members of the great nobility, Henry Bolingbroke and Thomas Mowbray, Duke of Norfolk. The two ended up accusing each other of treason to the king. Richard exiled them both and then, when Gaunt died in 1399, refused Bolingbroke, who was in France, entry into the Lancastrian estates. Bolingbroke was exiled for life.

While Richard was pursuing a difficult campaign in Ireland in 1399, Bolingbroke landed in eastern England from France with a hundred soldiers and marched westward toward Wales, intending to interrupt Richard's return to his stronghold in Chester. The lords and their retainers joined Bolingbroke in vast numbers. With very little fighting he put together a huge army as he moved across the country from east to west.

The magnates had come to think of Richard as not suitable to be king. His arbitrary attack on members of the higher nobility frightened them. He continued to surround himself with younger nobles who did not marry, or if they did, had, like Richard and his queen, Anne of Bohemia, no issue.

There appears to have been a homosexual coterie at the royal court. Richard seems to have had no interest in heterosexual behavior. After Anne died, he married a five-year-old daughter of the King of France partly for diplomatic reasons, but partly to avoid the marriage bed for many years.

By the time Richard had got his ships together and left Ireland with some of his army, his cause was lost, and he surrendered to Henry. A special parliament was called, headed by the magnates and London citizens. First they deposed Richard for unconstitutional acts (his claiming that the law was in his breast, illegal taxation, arbitrary judgment against Bolingbroke, and others). Then they acceded to Bolingbroke's claim to the throne (as one of the two closest claimants by blood, and the closest in the male line). Richard was taken to the

Tower of London and later was done away with at Pontefract Castle.

Richard II abdicated, but to make sure of his abjuration of the throne, the magnates saw to it that he was also deposed. The charges against Richard, which consisted of twenty-nine articles, do mention his sodomite behavior—to please the churchmen and perhaps further inflame the London populace against the King. Gaunt had seen disaster lurking, and he protected Richard even against his own son, Bolingbroke. After Gaunt came the deluge.

Gaunt believed in the sacred nature of anointment to the kingship. He believed in primogeniture, under which in 1377 Richard, the then ten-year-old son of Gaunt's elder brother Edward, had inherited the throne.

Undoubtedly Gaunt would have loved to wear the crown. But that was outside the realm of possibility. Above all, Gaunt was a Plantagenet who wanted to maintain the dignity of the bloodlines of his family.

What Gaunt would have thought if he had lived another eighteen months and witnessed his son Henry Bolingbroke usurp the throne with approval of Parliament is hard to say. Gaunt would certainly have had mixed feelings, and if Bolingbroke in exile in France had consulted his father on his plan to invade England and push his cousin off the throne, it is probable that Gaunt would have discouraged him.

Henry IV was a typical magnate, devoted to the hunt, politics, and the pursuit of women. He had gained fame,

probably undeserved, participating in a crusade against heathen Slavs on the eastern border of Germany. Bolingbroke
already had a son in 1399; that son, in 1413, would become
Henry V. The Lancastrians ruled until 1471, to be replaced
by the Yorkists.

Because of Bolingbroke's usurpation of the throne in
1399 with the approval of Parliament, Henry IV and his
Lancastrian successors were always gentle in their treatment
of Parliament, including the House of Commons.

The gentry and burgesses in Commons by 1450 were
asserting the "liberties of the House of Commons": freedom
of speech in Parliament, freedom from arrest while Parliament was in session, and freedom to decide on disputed elections to the House of Commons. The Lancastrian monarchy
ignored these radical demands. They were not realized until
the seventeenth century.

⁂

In the third volume of his three-volume *Constitutional History of England*, William Stubbs, Victorian Britain's greatest
medieval historian, postulated the existence of something he
called "the Lancastrian Constitution." From the accession of
Henry IV in 1399 until the replacement of the Lancastrian
dynasty by Edward IV of York in 1471, Stubbs saw operating
in England a constitutional system and principle in which
the king ruled in cooperation with Parliament, a foreshad-
owing of Britain's modern constitution.

Twentieth- and twenty-first-century historians have rejected Stubbs's protomodern Lancastrian Constitution. It is true that Henry IV, his son, and his grandson were sensitive to parliamentary power, but this is seen as a pragmatic development, not a course of action based on a constitutional principle.

Whether the Lancastrian Constitution was a pragmatic thing or was founded on enunciation of a protomodern principle, it predated 1399 and can be seen in John of Gaunt's careful and manipulative but nonauthoritarian dealings with Parliament, and especially the House of Commons. Gaunt played politics and sought to control elections and massaged the MPs. He avoided conflict with them as far as he could.

This fits in with our general picture of Gaunt as at bottom a moderate person who accepted the world he had been born into, sought to affect it at the margins, but never used his wealth and image to confront and change his world. He was open to new ideas but made his own liminal judgment as to how far he could go with these novelties. He loomed large on the public stage, but essentially he was a private person committed to his family. He was willing to acknowledge defeat and to compromise with reality. He was an enlightened and energetic aristocrat who lived at the dividing line between the Middle Ages and the Renaissance.

Gaunt knew that he was the beneficiary of good fortune and the blessings of history. But he also was aware of the social, political, and cultural contexts that limited what he could do with inherited wealth, status, and power. He was the model for successful elites in all times and places—courageous, literate, conscientious, but forever conscious of the limits to what great wealth and high station could achieve.

Politics is the distribution of power and of the benefits of power. Who gets what, where, when? Politics involves "the political nation," that is, the people who really count at a given time and who derive the benefits from the distribution of power. The political nation comprises opinion makers. They are the people whose cooperation and advice are needed by even the most authoritarian governments.

In Gaunt's time the political nation consisted of about 5 percent of the free male population. They were the lay and ecclesiastical lords and the Commons, members of Parliament who represented the upper stratum of the gentry, selected by the shire courts and by the merchant classes in the towns. Even as late as 1832, the date of the first Parliamentary Reform Act, the political nation was still circumscribed at 5 percent of the male population.

In 1376 England had sufficient bureaucrats that the government could have been administered centrally from London in an authoritarian manner. The slowness of communication presented a problem, but not an insuperable one. Yet Gaunt chose to deal with the obstreperous Commons in a mild way. He simply manipulated the electoral system to get MPs who would do his bidding in 1378.

In 1376 he could have dismissed Parliament angrily and

hunted down and harassed the MPs. He chose not to pursue this draconian method partly because his temperament was one of caution and accommodation. But that was not the only reason for his moderate behavior.

The key here was the framework of the common law. By this time there was well entrenched in England a system of circuit judges, grand juries, "petty" juries in criminal cases, and juries in civil (property) actions as well as in the fast-developing areas of "torts" or liability.

The political system of Parliamentary government was connected to this judicial system. Gaunt could not dismiss the Commons and hunt them down and punish them without raising misgivings in society about the stability of the common law. The shire court was the key institution that embraced both politics and law. It was the court of first jurisdiction for civil and criminal actions, and also the place where MPs were elected. In both law and politics there was a significant level of autonomy and corporate self-government. Whatever his personal feelings may have been, Gaunt could not challenge this interconnected system.

CHAPTER TEN

Chaucer

J OHN OF GAUNT EMBODIED the culmination of medieval chivalric culture. This cultural mode was put into verse in the *Book of the Duchess,* the elegy on Gaunt's first wife, Blanche, the White Duchess. The poem was written by Geoffrey Chaucer (d. 1400), who wrote under Lancaster's patronage.

Gaunt gave a pension to Chaucer early in the poet's career and saw to it that important and remunerative government posts came Chaucer's way: collector of customs in the port of London, and at least two embassies on the Continent, to France and northern Italy. Chaucer's wife, Philippa, also received a small pension from Gaunt's largesse.

Chaucer was born to a prosperous but not very wealthy London family. His father was a wine merchant. The Chaucers lived in the heart of bourgeois London. Close to their house was a prep school established by the Inns of Court, the training school for the legal profession. The prep schools run by the Inns of Court were for young students, as young as fourteen, who were chosen by their gentry and merchant families to be trained to become barristers. Lawyers did not attend a university; that was for future ecclesiastics.

It is possible that Chaucer received a humanistic education at a prep school run by one of these Inns of Court. And it was a sterling education. Chaucer could write poetry in either French or English; he almost single-handedly made English a literary language. He could read Latin and Italian and probably spoke Italian fluently.

Chaucer read Dante's *Divine Comedy* closely, as he did the *Romance of the Rose,* the French chivalric poem. He was very much taken with Giovanni Boccaccio, the Florentine writer, whose narrative poems Chaucer translated and expanded upon. Chaucer was familiar with the work of Petrarch, the poet and ideologist of the Florentine humanistic Renaissance. On his embassy to northern Italy Chaucer may have sought out and conversed with Petrarch.

What drew Gaunt to Chaucer was first of all that the poet could write in English on courtly themes. Heretofore only French and Italian poets had expatiated on courtliness and chivalry. But Chaucer could do the same in an English language that was increasingly being given literary form and was becoming acceptable among the aristocracy not only in daily discourse but as a medium for expressing those literary themes that had been central to the mind-set of the aristocracy since the late twelfth century.

Chaucer had in fact a very competent competitor for the role of England's preeminent poet. In the 1370s and '80s an anonymous member of the gentry living a hundred miles north of Oxford wrote two remarkable poems: *Pearl* and *Sir Gawain and the Green Knight.*

The first was the elegy on the death of a young girl discussed earlier. The second was a French-style romantic epic. These poems were written in a provincial dialect different from Chaucer's. It was Chaucer who prevailed in the public eye because he wrote in the London vernacular, he had access to the royal court to read his poems, and he had the patronage of John of Gaunt. The *Gawain* poet's single manuscript containing the two poems (and two others) remained in obscurity until the twentieth century.

Another reason Gaunt was drawn to Chaucer was that the poet was working at the leading edge of European culture, drawing from Italian neoclassical humanistic genres as well as from French romance. Chaucer was an up-to-date metropolitan poet writing in the London dialect and reflecting the new literary and intellectual trends coming from northern Italy. If you were an aristocrat in late-fourteenth-century England, you would, like Gaunt, bet on supporting Chaucer. He had all the qualities needed to attract artistic patronage. Some critics today think that the *Gawain* poet was close to being Chaucer's equal as a writer. But Chaucer, thanks in part to Gaunt, had the impact and visibility.

Chaucer imbibed the principles of the Florentine

humanistic school, its devotion to the classics, its greater consciousness of the individual than was found in Anglo-French romance. These Renaissance cultural trends were embedded in Chaucer's first great masterpiece, *Troilus and Criseyde*. He worked on this romantic narrative for six years, completing it in 1382.

It is the first great love poem in the English language. It tells the story of the love of Troilus and Criseyde, who live among the aristocratic class in Troy in its later days. Introduced by Criseyde's uncle, they fall passionately in love, and the first part of the poem blazes with erotic love expressed in a frank and quite physical mode. But the wheel of fortune turns: family and politics intervene to interrupt their love, which ends in bitterness and tragedy.

Within the traditional framework of the chivalric romance, Chaucer created a psychological masterpiece, closely exploring the feelings and passions of the two lovers. *Troilus and Criseyde* exhibits a new humanistic realism and consciousness of the interior life of the individual. As one writer explains, "We read Chaucer's masterpiece as a triumph over the medieval, a breakthrough into the literature of objective representation and ironic distancing, into the modern." (D. R. Howard, *Chaucer, His Life, His Works, His World.*)

The last decade of Chaucer's life and work was taken up with writing *The Canterbury Tales*. In contrast to *Troilus and Criseyde*, it was a sociological panorama rather than a psychological probing. Chaucer did not live to complete his most popular work, but he laid out the complex structure and built part of it before his death.

A group of pilgrims are going from a tavern in Southwark in London to Canterbury. To pass the time on the long trip, they decide that each of them will tell two stories on each leg of the trip. The stories are popular ones, expressed in the language of the commoners. "Whan that Aprille with his shoures soote / The droghte of Marche hath perced to the roote . . . / Than longen folk to goon on pilgrimages," from "The Prologue," are some of the most recognizable lines in English literature.

Some stories in *The Canterbury Tales* are religious (including anti-Semitic tales); some are bawdy; some express the highest degree of chivalry. Chaucer creates a mosaic of middle-class people, carefully articulated by their language and favorite fictions. Among them is a great comic character, the Wife of Bath, who looked upon serial marriages as a natural right for survival and prosperity. She had had five husbands, and she wore a headdress that weighed a full ten pounds, red stockings, and spurs.

The Knight was a worthy man who loved high chivalry, truth, honor, freedom, and courtesy. He was a very perfect gentle knight.

The Nun (Prioress) was coy, liked to chant the Divine Services, spoke fair French, and wiped her upper lip so clean that not a speck of grease could be seen on the rim of her cup. She wore a brooch engraved *Amor vincit omnia* (Love conquers all).

The Monk rode a very expensive horse, wore fine boots, and had fur on the edge of his sleeves. He never understood why monks were supposed to stay in the cloister all day and do nothing but read. He had a stable full of greyhounds and rode to the hunt.

The Friar knew well the taverns in every shire. He thought that it wasn't worth his time to worry about those who had to beg their bread. He kept in touch with richer folk and believed that the true sign of repentance was a gift to humble friars such as himself.

The Oxford Scholar spent his money on books rather than food. He was full of high ideals and virtue, and "gladly would he learn, and gladly teach."

The Lawyer knew all the laws and could pick flaws out of wills for a fee, but yet "he seemed busier than he was."

The Physician was pompous, rich, and wise. He gave the druggist trade with his prescriptions, and "each brisk business for the other made." He loved gold.

The Miller, a thickset lout, was a champion wrestler. His beard was fiery red and he had a wart with bristly hairs on his nose. He was vulgar and he told the bawdiest tale in the bunch.

The Summoner, whose duties were to search and bring to court offenders against the Church, had a red face and scared the children with his blotched and pimpled skin, little piglike eyes, and beardless chin. He smelled of garlic and onions. He shouted Latin phrases he didn't understand. "For like a parrot he was really dense; / He'd learned the words, but could not grasp the sense."

The Pardoner carried a wallet full of pardons hot from Rome, had stringy blond hair, and knew that he had to preach a fine sermon in order to get the silver to tinkle in the plate.

The Parson was learned, wise, and true. He was a gentle priest who paid the church taxes himself for the poor parishioners who couldn't afford them. He traveled from one town to the next. As a minister, he felt he had to set an example for his flock. "No wonder that iron rots if gold should rust!" was one of his favorite lines. The Parson was one of Chaucer's favorite characters. In "The Prologue," Chaucer says he was "a Christian both in deed and thought. / He lived himself the Golden Rule he taught." (Translated by J. S. P. Tatlock and Percy MacKay in *The Complete Poetical Works of Geoffrey Chaucer.*)

These are some of the pilgrims who set out on that fine April day to tell their stories between Southwark and Canterbury. The stories all fit the characters of their tellers, in theme, language, and substance. This represents the first great comedic work of literature in the English of the day, vastly changed from the English of *Beowulf,* written in the eighth century.

⌇⌇⌇

In the *Book of the Duchess,* Chaucer wrote fully in accordance with the chivalric tradition. He and Gaunt would have been at one on depicting the idealized persons and motifs of the culture of chivalry. *Troilus and Criseyde* retains the framework of chivalric romance but undermines courtly love conventions and aristocratic gestures by its cleverly articulated psychological realism. My guess is that Gaunt would have liked the highly charged eroticism of the first part of the poem, but would have been made uneasy by the psychological probing and sadness of the later sections.

Gaunt would probably have been dismayed that *The Canterbury Tales* dealt with the middle- and lower-class people whom he frequently encountered but never gave much thought to, but he undoubtedly would have enjoyed some of the stories, particularly "The Miller's Tale" and "The Knight's Tale," for totally different reasons. They embodied the two facets of Gaunt's character—his bawdiness and courtliness.

Chaucer's pictures of his Canterbury pilgrims are obviously to be seen in a comedic light. Here Chaucer was much influenced by Giovanni Boccacio's *Decameron,* which depicts middle-class Florentines in a similar risible manner.

But there is always a ribbon of sadness and pessimism running through comedy. Chaucer's people are, for the most part, deeply flawed, and it is their flaws that make them interesting to us.

There is a sadness to all this. These middle-class people are immobile on the social scale. They will achieve nothing; they have no future different from the messy middle-class present. *The Canterbury Tales* can be taken as a picture of stagnant bourgeois behavior, corrupt and morally wretched, a world full of self-hatred and useless anxiety.

In this way, Chaucer presents an aristocratic view of his people. Gaunt would have agreed with the futility and damage described, except that, unlike Chaucer, he would never have bothered to contemplate these middle-class people close up. Nor would the Duke have considered them an appropriate subject for poetry.

George Williams in *A New View of Chaucer* (1965), has proposed that, at least in their earlier years, Philippa, John of Gaunt, and Catherine Swynford lived as a *ménage à trois*. Philippa had a daughter by John of Gaunt while Gaunt was at the same time involved with Catherine Swynford (fathering four children by her). Williams claims that Geoffrey Chaucer, who by his own testimony had an unhappy marriage, lived mostly separated from his wife, Philippa, John of Gaunt's initial mistress. Williams also suggests that the mysterious Thomas Chaucer, Geoffrey Chaucer's nominal son, was actually the product of a union between the Duke and Philippa Chaucer.

Williams proposes that in the poem *Troilus and Criseyde*, Chaucer devised an allegory beseeching Gaunt not to desert his mistress Catherine by going to Spain for several years. (He did go.) What Chaucer got out of the arrangement was patronage, financial assistance, a sinecure in the customs administration, and for a decade or more a rent-free house in the center of London.

Williams has no proof of this lascivious conduct toward the two sisters, Philippa Chaucer and Catherine Swynford, but it does lie within the realm of possibility. Chaucer's most recent biographer, Derek Pearsall, a strict constructionist, barely mentions Catherine Swynford. The thought of the Duke having his way with the two sisters is something Pearsall never suggests. It is, however, an interesting possible perspective on Gaunt's behavior, and on Chaucer as the beneficiary of his wife's indiscretions.

That Gaunt was much more lavish in his patronage of Chaucer in the poet's earlier years than his later years indicates that Gaunt realized clearly that Chaucer had departed from traditional chivalric culture and courtly love toward new horizons of sensibility. The older Gaunt must have felt himself intellectually limited and psychologically superseded when he read about the Trojan lovers or the Canterbury pilgrims or listened as the poems were read after dinner in aristocratic circles.

In his lifetime, a long span by the standards of his age and class, John of Gaunt encountered three forces that loomed on the European horizon as the shape of the future. Rebellious peasants were one of these new forces; Gaunt was a bogeyman for them. Parliamentary institutions involving representation of the rural and urban upper middle class were another force, also for a time directed against Gaunt. Though he overcame this opposition by manipulating the election of the knights of the shire, he was not friendly with the more outspoken leaders of the Commons; intrinsically he had little respect for them.

The third force, religious reform, was initially more tempting to him, hence his early support for John Wyclif. But Gaunt backed off from his support for Wyclif. He sensed that Lancastrian alliance with the Lollards portended changes too drastic for state and society, as then constituted, to absorb. He quenched the spiritual thirst common in his generation in an entirely conventional manner, by giving his support to an austere order of monks.

Chaucer is somewhat like Wyclif in Gaunt's life. Gaunt's early patronage resulted in Chaucer's first long poem, an elegy on Gaunt's first wife. This energetic book remained entirely within the framework of traditional chivalric literature. When the psychological and sociological thrust of Chaucer's later work seemed remote and unexpected to Gaunt, he reduced his support for the poet.

Gaunt was a man of the aristocratic Anglo-French Middle Ages. He did not feel comfortable in the new intellectual world of the Renaissance.

◇▩▩◇

What brought about a cultural revolution in the fifteenth century was the extension of the privileged circumstances enjoyed by Gaunt and his peers to a wealthy middle class. From their ranks rose the new poets and philosophers—or the patrons of the new poets and philosophers.

"The urgency of examining the ideology sustaining individualism under conditions of generalized wealth and leisure in the West" (Ingrid Wassenaar) was to set the social and cultural foundations for the Renaissance. A similar social change was to make for the cultural revolution of modernism in the early years of the twentieth century. Proust's world was fashioned out of an expansion of wealth and leisure similar to that which engendered Petrarch's world.

This new individualism made its way into *Troilus and Criseyde* and *The Canterbury Tales* and separated Chaucer from his patron John of Gaunt. Gaunt was the refined embodiment of the old knightly world that had prevailed since the twelfth century. Chaucer was looking to new horizons of humanism.

The development of consciousness and the arts and intellectual growth in general are dependent on the security and privilege accorded to certain individuals of extraordinary sensibility. This social crux is what marked the relationship between Gaunt and Chaucer. That is why Gaunt's patronage of Chaucer was so important for the beginnings of Renaissance literature in England. The old aristocrat gave the poet the peace and leisure to express a new consciousness.

The first ingredient of the new consciousness was a changed and more intensive attitude to the classical heritage. There had been two previous eras of deep interest in the classical heritage in the Middle Ages. The first era was the Carolingian renaissance from 780 to 850. The second was the twelfth-century renaissance from about 1140 to 1240. But in both instances cultivation of the classical heritage was closely bound up with Christian ideas. Indeed, the leading exponents of classicism in the ninth and twelfth centuries were clerics.

The Renaissance that began in the late fourteenth century and in which Chaucer played a leading part was secular. *Troilus and Criseyde* takes place in ancient Troy and it does not involve Christianity. It is a humanistic—non-religious—probing of psychological and sexual relationships, free from Christian guilt and Christian comfort.

A second ingredient of the new consciousness was urbanism, an interest in town life and the characters that develop in an urban environment, their hopes, aspirations, limitations, and disappointments. The potential of urban middle-class culture and the strains upon it—this is expounded in *The Canterbury Tales*. Whatever else Chaucer had in mind in his great unfinished poem, the novel vistas of urban life and the strengths and weaknesses of middle-class living in towns was a prominent theme he was exploring.

"Chaucer's commonwealth is implicitly utopian . . . in its opening of existing hierarchies to infiltration by new classes of people." (Paul Strohm, *Social Chaucer.*) John of Gaunt was a good literary critic: he recognized the subversive implications of Chaucer's later work.

CHAPTER ELEVEN

The End of the Middle Ages

THE CONVENTIONAL WAY to write history is to make horizontal temporal divisions in the past. That means history is divided into periods. That is how history is taught to college freshmen. It is how the history section of a chain bookstore is divided.

These periods tend to get shorter as they approach the present, like sections of a folding telescope. The dating of the first three eras in European history—Antiquity, the Middle Ages, and the Renaissance—is generally held as 3500 B.C. to about A.D. 450; 450 to 1400; and then 1400 to 1550. This periodization would be followed by the Reformation and then the Enlightenment. However, the time from 1400 to 1750 is often nowadays compacted into one era, that of Early Modern times.

The conventional horizontal division of the past has seemed naïve and boring to the French school of the Annales, which arose in the 1930s and is still active. How can it be said, goes the Annales argument, that 1400 ended the Middle Ages and began the Renaissance? Given the continuity of society and thought, such periodization is naïve and artificial. Challenged to develop an alternative to the conventional approach, the Annales school propounded a vertical rather than horizontal division of history.

In the 1960s and '70s it became fashionable for historians, led by the French scholar Fernand Braudel, to talk about the "long duration" in European history. This view had first been postulated in the 1930s by Marc Bloch, and it was held to be particularly germane to the rural working class.

Bloch and Braudel claimed that the peasantry in France changed very little between 1300 and 1750. Kings and lords came and went and intellectual and religious fashions underwent some development, but looking at the 60 percent of the population that formed the rural working class, for the mass base of French society, durability, not change, was the historical pattern.

It was not until the Industrial Revolution and its attendant urbanization that a new era really began, at first in Britain more than in France. The Middle Ages, in short, extended into the late eighteenth century. Only then did a new era start and a new modern, industrial, urbanized civilization emerge.

There is certainly something persuasive in this long-duration view of European history. In novels like *Far From the Madding Crowd* and *The Return of the Native*, published in the

1880s, Thomas Hardy depicted scenes of English rural working-class life that could have occurred in the fifteenth century.

The weakness of the Bloch-Braudel long-duration thesis of European history, its extension of the Middle Ages into the eighteenth century, is that it looks at civilization too much from the bottom up. It gives strong priority to the history of the peasantry over that of other classes and groups in society. It gives primacy to economic and social history over intellectual, cultural, and political change. When these other facets of civilization are considered, the Middle Ages indeed substantially ended, at least in England, around 1400, about the time John of Gaunt died. Gaunt was the last of the medieval knights in any cultural and psychological sense.

In politics, the abdication, deposition, and murder of Gaunt's nephew, Richard II, to be replaced by Richard's cousin and Gaunt's son, Henry Bolingbroke, signaled the end of medieval monarchy. Shakespeare got it right. Once the balm was washed off an anointed king and inheritance of the crown by bloodline was no longer honored, national politics changed.

The basis of monarchy was now popular support, along with the maintenance of the goodwill of the political classes represented in Parliament. That was the reason why Henry IV (r. 1399–1413) was such a nervous and mediocre king; he was not sure of his mandate. Gaunt's grandson Henry V (r. 1413–1422) won popular victories in France. Military glory renewed the popularity and increased the strength of the monarchy.

But Gaunt's great-grandson Henry VI (r. 1422–1461 and 1470–1471) turned out to be feeble and half mad due to a bad gene inherited from the French king who was Henry VI's maternal grandfather. Henry VI lost control of the monarchy to the Yorkist rivals of the now enfeebled Lancastrians. Parliament came to play a major role in the stability of the royal government.

Parliament was used in the 1530s by Henry VIII (r. 1509–1547), descendant of both Lancastrians and Yorkists, to carry out the beginning of the Reformation in England and the split with Rome. What Gaunt could have accomplished in the 1370s by supporting Wyclif, Henry VIII achieved, opening the way to Lutheranism and Calvinism, and the stripping of the Catholic altars.

By 1590 England was a Protestant nation, and that meant a world of difference in church organization, political thought, piety and religious ritual, and popular culture. That in 1590 90 percent of the population was divided among Anglicans of the Established Church and various temperaments of the Calvinist communities and some even more radical sects, one or two descended from the Lollards of Wyclif's and Gaunt's time, does not modify the conclusion that a religious, intellectual, and political revolution was precipitated by Henry VIII's break with Rome.

The medieval Church, which played such a major role in the life of the English people, from images in their churches, to their language and literature, to their reliance on faith healing as the prime form of medicine, had been interrupted and proven to be not durable.

Since the 1940s Protestantism of the Calvinist and more radical varieties has received a bad press among British historians and their American followers. But the Reformation of the sixteenth century was the great dividing line in English and Scottish history before the Industrial Revolution. It deeply affected all aspects of life, not least by giving the English and Scottish people the sense that they were chosen by God to conquer and populate the world.

The roots of Protestantism go back to Gaunt's lifetime. It was never entirely eradicated, and Henry VIII's split with Rome—ostensibly to make an honest woman of his pregnant mistress—gave the remnants of Lollardy the opportunity to join up with the imported Lutheranism and Calvinism and over the course of a century to change England and Scotland into Protestant nations.

This view of British history was popular in the late nineteenth and early twentieth centuries. It is denigrated today, when medieval Catholicism has become so popular among historians, but the truth of the older view cannot be denied and will slowly be reasserted.

It doesn't matter in the long run that in the 1560s many of the common people held on desperately to the Holy Rood (Cross of Christ), the old sacraments, their saints for every occasion, and their now rapidly aging Catholic parish priests. By 1620, except for outlying manor houses and villages, mostly in the north, the whole bag and baggage of the medieval Church was in the process of being swept away.

Efforts made by the conservative High Church wing of the Anglican Church in the seventeenth and nineteenth centuries to recover some of the old medieval ways of religion would have only limited and temporary success.

It was only with the massive Irish Catholic immigration to England in the nineteenth and twentieth centuries that a renewed, strong Roman Catholic Church emerged again in England. By the 1950s and '60s Irish Catholics had penetrated into the ranks of fashionable historians at Oxford, Cambridge, and other leading universities. Then began the process, still ongoing, of denigrating Protestantism and diminishing the importance of the Reformation.

Yet when the Catholic altars were stripped in the sixteenth century, Protestant pulpits by and large took their place. From these pulpits was preached liberty of conscience, an antipathy to ritual and religious art, a more egalitarian and democratic view of humanity, and separation of church and state—convictions that were pursued intensely in the American colonies. These articles of faith were far removed from John of Gaunt's world.

ᴑᴛᴛᴛᴚꝺ

Gaunt's world was also in the course of being superseded in a military sense. By 1400 the heavily armored knight fighting on horseback was becoming obsolete. Gaunt's grandson

Henry V won the Battle of Agincourt in 1415 by putting up six thousand infantry, lightly armored and wielding long-bows and pikes, to break the charge of French knighthood. By midcentury the use of cannons would make obsolete as well the walling of towns and traditional siege warfare.

There were still aristocrats in burnished armor to lead armies, but by 1500 the important military component was the mercenary foot soldier, by 1600 also wielding a musket. How many foot soldiers could you afford to recruit and how well would you train and arm them? That became the crucial military question. How many armored knights you could put in the field on expensive horses became steadily less impor-tant. Gaunt was part of an awesome military system, founded around 800, that was at last losing its importance in war and society.

The English Tudor monarchs of the late fifteenth and six-teenth centuries postured and pretended, but they knew they did not have the means to put an army on the Continent. After the victories and turmoil of the Hundred Years' War and the romantic victories of Edward III, the Black Prince, and Henry V, England was an insignificant military power in the sixteenth century. Military leadership passed to the French kings and the Austrian and Spanish Hapsburg emperors.

France had three or four times the population of England and could put infantry armies into the field that far out-numbered what England's puny population, not recovered from the Black Death, could provide. The Hapsburgs used gold and silver from Spain's American colonies to arm and equip millions of mercenaries drawn from central Europe and Belgium.

It took the fanatical Protestant Oliver Cromwell in the mid-seventeenth century to teach the English how to employ infantry. He also gave England an edge in warfare over the Hapsburgs, the French, and the Dutch by creating a navy that became predominant in the English Channel and on the great seas. To Cromwell, John of Gaunt would have seemed like a foolish relic from a distant past.

For most of his life John of Gaunt was in the vanguard, not only of fashion and lifestyle, but also of values. His avowal and cultivation of chivalry, courtly love, and decent treatment of highborn women; his loyalty to his difficult nephew Richard II out of respect for monarchy; his patronage of friars and poets; his personal bravery and military skills; his love of tournaments and the hunt; even his benign treatment of his mistress who became his third wife, and his devotion to his progeny both legitimate and illegitimate—all these put him at the forefront of the aristocracy of his day. But in the end, he resisted the coming of the new age of the Renaissance.

Where the Renaissance humanism differed from the culture of the Middle Ages was in four areas. It was more sensitive to and realistic about the complexities of individual psychology. It was more receptive to bourgeois ways of living and thinking. It had an enhanced respect for classical antiquity, its philosophy, literature, and art forms. It attributed new importance to vernacular language and generated high-quality vernacular literature, at the same time as its scholars refurbished medieval Latinity and made it more classical in style.

Ever since 1860, when Jacob Burckhardt published *The Civilization of the Renaissance in Italy*—the first book to argue that 1400 was the turning point at which a new individualism replaced medieval group thinking—historians have debated what caused the Renaissance or even whether or not it could be distinguished from the Middle Ages.

Those who believe in a novel and distinctive Renaissance culture point to many roots: the growth of cities, the commercial capitalist expansion, the formation of bureaucratic states, the rise of a highly literate as well as wealthy upper middle class, the improvement in education at the primary and secondary levels, the genius of Petrarch and Chaucer, who compelled new ways of thinking.

All these factors were in play, but perhaps the most important cause for the rise of Renaissance humanism was the exhaustion of the refined and hitherto creative medieval aristocratic culture itself.

The world of John of Gaunt was founded around 800. Its center was the great families, the billionaire landlords who dominated society, state, and church. Within and around the great families there developed a distinctive culture, whether exemplified in chivalry, strict class differentiation, or university learning. By 1400 it had exhausted itself. It was lacking in new ideas. Its zenith was in the life and mind of John of Gaunt. Confronted with new ideas in the person of Wyclif, a religious and social revolution, and a cultural revolution in the later writings of Chaucer, Gaunt and his culture were at sea.

Gaunt stayed with the world with which he was familiar—the world of high consumption, knighthood, and aristocratic power. In this conservatism he resembled the American billionaires of today. Like them, Gaunt and his peers were satisfied with the world as they knew it. They thought history had stopped.

⌒〰〰⌒

But history does not stop. Its advance, for better or worse, is inexorable, whether in the aristocratic world of Gaunt or the liberal capitalist world of today. Beneath the secure surface, fissures in culture, politics, and society will appear, and they will alter the structure in unpredictable ways.

After John of Gaunt's time, the Protestant Reformation, by undermining the unity and authority of the Catholic Church, greatly strengthened the power and efficiency of Catholicism's long-standing competitor, the monarchical and republican administrative state. At least this is what happened in England. And all over Western Europe in the fifteenth century, the middle class became more politically active and more central to national wealth, culture, and politics.

In Italy the families of the merchant princes took over urban governments and patronage of the arts. In England the gentry increased in size, wealth, and political influence. As Chaucer had anticipated, a more rational and sophisticated consciousness, abetted by neoclassical trends in education, became steadily more central to national culture. There was increased polarization in peasant society, between the entrepreneurial yeoman class and the land-starved ordinary farmers.

While Chaucer readily grasped the significance of Renaissance humanism's capacity for a more modern psychological insight, and William Langland's poem expressed submerged proletarian rumblings, no visionary could possibly have anticipated all these changes from Gaunt's world.

Yet many aspects of Gaunt's world lived on. There is still an aristocracy in England. Today the billionaire capitalists in Britain, the United States, and Canada perpetuate much of the Lancastrian lifestyle. The fancy town house, the country estate, all kinds of conspicuous consumption, including very expensive dinner parties, close attention to dress and furnishings, and armed bodyguards—the social elite still lives some of the more visible aspects of the Lancastrian mode.

Another way in which the billionaire capitalists of today perpetuate Gaunt's lifestyle is in patronage of the arts. While in Europe since World War II, governments have been the prime (but not exclusive) patrons of the arts, in America, opera companies, symphony orchestras, and the visual arts would shrink to pitiable condition without the kind of aristocratic patronage that Gaunt practiced.

Two of Gaunt's English descendants in the fifteenth century were particularly prominent in continuing the Lancastrian tradition of patronage of arts and learning. A grandson, the military man John, Duke of Bedford, commissioned and collected French illuminated manuscripts whose artwork stands at the zenith of late medieval accomplishment in painting. A great-grandson, Humphrey, Duke of Gloucester, built up an impressive library that was eventually incorporated into the Bodleian Library at Oxford University. The Bodleian's medieval manuscript room is still called Duke Humphrey's Library.

Graduate students at Oxford still enter Duke Humphrey's Library in awe. In 1993 the Society of Antiquaries of London published a large book that was an inventory of the artworks in John of Bedford's collection, from silver salt cellars to French books of hours, illuminated manuscripts that are now virtually priceless.

At the same time, the other side of the legacy of John of Gaunt through his descendants would not be forgotten—his arrogance, militarism, and lack of compassion for the poor and the downtrodden. Another of his grandsons, Henry the Navigator, Prince of Portugal, can be regarded as the principal founder of the African slave trade's place in European overseas expansion.

The African slave trade turned out to be easy to implement and administer and immensely profitable. The black chieftains in Africa had long cooperated with Muslim Arab slave traders. Now they cooperated with the Arabs' Christian Portuguese successors. The initial use of black slaves in sugar plantations in the Portuguese Azores turned out to be effective.

Soon, however, zealous friars began to question whether the slavery of black Africans and their servitude under the lash conformed to the ideals of Christian civilization, and whether the royal family of Portugal should itself take such a prominent role in African slavery, considering the claims of the royal family to be moral exemplars for their people.

Prince Henry the Navigator's reply to these difficult questions would be along the following lines, veering from attitudes of a Christian aristocrat of the Middle Ages toward modern racism, which took root in Spain and Portugal in the late fifteenth century:

> The Archbishop of Lisbon and the royal councillors tell me that we should have no qualms about our involvement with the slave trade. In the first place, these Africans are heathens and are condemned to hell. But even should they convert to the Catholic faith, that would not affect their status and labor in this world.
>
> St. Paul said that slaves as well as freemen may enter the Church and from there the Kingdom of Heaven,

but neither Paul nor Jesus, our Savior Himself, nor the Church Fathers, like Ambrose and Augustine, questioned the existence of slavery in the Roman empire in which they lived.

In this world the Heavenly and Earthly City are in conflict, but only God knows the membership of these communities. So we have a right to go on with our social institutions, one of which is slavery.

Jesus said that the poor will enter the Kingdom of Heaven. But He had nothing to say about slaves. Anyway, He meant the poor in spirit, which can include lords as well as peasants.

Slavery is part of the way of life of our Christian society. Slavery was part of the way of life of the ancient Romans, both pagans and Christians. There are no grounds for questioning the morality of slavery.

You also have to consider who these African people are. They are people with black skins. Blackness is a sign of shame. These Africans bear the mark of Cain. There must be something wrong with them, some terrible crime their forefathers committed.

We know that whiteness of skin is a sign of goodness. We have moral superiority over these Africans. We have a God-given right to dominate them and exploit their labor. My grandfather, John of Gaunt, Duke of Lancaster, like the other English lords, had very white skin and blond hair. I am proud of that.

How fortunate it was that Duke John's daughter Philippa, my mother, married into the Portuguese royal line. That gave something special to Portuguese princes, like myself. That is why I am fair-haired, like my grandfather, John of Gaunt.

The fairness of my skin and hair marks me and some members of my family as separate from most Iberians. The skin of most Portuguese and Spaniards is swarthy; their hair is dark.

The Iberians are a product of two eras of race mixture. Our Visigoth ancestors who conquered Iberia from the Romans in the fifth century were like the Germans and Scandinavians from whom they derived. Their skin was white and their hair was blond or red. But the Roman population of Iberia was a mixture of all the many peoples of the great Roman empire—Italians, Greeks, Berbers from North Africa, and the original inhabitants who went back many centuries before Rome.

When the Christian princes came out of their northern mountain redoubts and conquered most of Iberia in the thirteenth century, they conquered a population of millions of Muslim Arabs and Berbers and Jews. The friars were eager to convert the Arabs and Jews to our Christian faith. With the help of Christian kings and lords that was not hard to do. Half of the Arabs and Jews were converted to the true faith. The friars were happy, but this was a big mistake because now another race mixture occurred in Iberia.

That is why the Iberian people are a mixture of many folks, many nations, and why most Iberians have a swarthy skin and dark hair. And to think that many of the Jewish convert families are secretly Marranos, who subversively practice their Jewish faith—in secret they light candles on Friday night; they disdain the eating of pigs.

How proud I am to be directly descended from a blond and white-skinned Englishman, my grandfather John of Gaunt.

One thing we must be careful about when we import black African slaves to work our estates. If they become Christian, as the reckless friars wish, we must take care not to allow intermarriage of our Iberian peasants with these black people. That would be yet a third stage of race mixture in the history of Christian Iberia.

We are not a pure people. We are not white and fair-haired like our Germanic Visigothic ancestors. Now we have Arab and Jewish blood in many of our families. We must forever guard against the intrusion of black African blood.

What had begun as a defense of aristocratic status eventually turned into racist imperialism. What was initiated as a culture of domination by certain great families turned into belief in the superiority of Western European genetic makeup. What had been feudalism became an idea of inherent superiority. What had been earned due to skill in tournament and on the battlefield became a belief in innate advantage.

The figure of John of Gaunt with his blond hair and reddish beard, a gift from his Viking heritage, became a claim and impetus to European domination of the world.

Medieval aristocracy was in origin and for a long time a pragmatic thing. Aristocracy emerged out of the later Carolingian empire around A.D. 800. It was shaped by politics, law, and economics and sustained by property, religion, and arts. It was a fighting man's and rich man's ethos.

After 1200, aristocracy was pacified, civilized, and feminized. It now had strongly cultural and intellectual qualities. By the fifteenth century there was consciousness of the value and specialty of aristocratic bloodlines.

Gaunt bought into this genetic ethos only modestly. Otherwise he would not have married his mistress, a commoner and an alien, started a new family with her, and legitimated this bastard family. But with Gaunt's grandson Prince Henry the Navigator, an intensified biological principle entered aristocratic idealism.

The Plantagenet aristocratic culture always had the potential to turn into racism. In the eleventh-century *Song of Roland,* a favorite of the Anglo-French aristocracy, the worst Muslims by far, the most fearsome, are the black Moors from Morocco. In accounts of the Norman Conquest of England in 1066, written by Anglo-Norman monastic chroniclers thirty or forth years after the Conquest, there is an underlying tone of racism. The French won because they were a superior people. The English were effete and decadent. The French knight on horseback with his chain mail and his lance was superior to the old-fashioned, superseded English, who had not learned to fight on horseback.

Froissart's account of the Hundred Years' War, describing two great early English victories led by Edward III and the Black Prince, has some of the same implicit racism. The French aristocracy lost because they were decadent, over-refined, lacking in personal toughness.

But it was left to Gaunt's grandson, Prince Henry of Portugal, to turn this Plantagenet implicit racism into state policy in support of the black slave trade and lay the foundation for the modern imperialist era to succeed the medieval aristocratic age.

⁂

The Lancastrian legacy was thus ambiguous. And this ambiguity has continued to characterize European civilization—and that of the United States—to the present day. Since the seventeenth century in England and continuing through the French Revolution and many revolutionary movements of the twentieth century, strenuous efforts have been made to eliminate ambiguity in favor of a common set of egalitarian revolutionary principles.

The results have not been fortunate. The efforts at revolutionary coordination produced in the twentieth century death and suffering on an unprecedented scale. On the other hand, under the guise of free markets and globalization, the current holders of wealth and power, the American billionaire capitalists, have reasserted the virtues of social ambiguity.

The billionaire capitalists have reasserted the position that social dichotomies and polarities are natural and acceptable. Social equality has been claimed by the great majority of university professors to be a chimera. The intellectual tide in the late twentieth and early twenty-first centuries is all in the direction of acceptance of social inequality as a fixed condition of the economic system

In the period from 1930 to 1975, Richard Henry Tawney, the economic historian and chief ideologist of the British Labour Party, and Rodney Hilton, a socialist historian of the medieval peasantry, posited a vision of social and economic equality. Tawney and Hilton attributed these conditions to medieval peasant communities, and they anticipated that an egalitarian mode would emerge again at some future date.

This socialist vision has turned to ashes. Christopher Dyer, the most recent authoritative historian of medieval peasantry, in his *Making a Living in the Middle Ages* (2002), states that the peasantry had "abandoned the attempt, in 1381, to seek to change the social and political structure from the outside."

So today it is believed that the present and future, as well as the past, must yield to the mechanics of a market-driven economy and the dictates of the billionaire capitalists. Tawney and Hilton lived in a socialist dream world. In contrast, it is now widely accepted that the class divisions in society are perpetually cruel and unchallengeable.

Wealth and poverty alongside one another; learning and high culture alongside ignorance and illiteracy; fashion and feasting alongside dirt and hunger; boisterous health alongside epidemic disease—these polarities constitute a return to the spirit of Gaunt's medieval world. The dream of leveling out that was inspired by twentieth-century modernization has now been abandoned for a kind of sardonic Lancastrian ideology.

Braudel and Bloch got it half right. There is a long duration in history. But it lies not in working-class life and thought. It lies in the consciousness and behavior of the ruling class.

In the twentieth century we were supposed to get away from a traditional ruling class. Modernization was supposed to make revolution—of the left or the right—possible. That did not occur in any durable sense.

A left-wing revolution occurred in Russia. The Bolsheviks blew away not only the czarist regime and aristocratic society and the wealthy merchant class but the rudiments of a liberal democracy. The Communist Party, representing the peasants and the urban workers, was supposed to make a new start in Russian history. The antique, heavily stratified class system would be eliminated and Russia would move rapidly toward being a highly industrialized society that would benefit the working class on whose behalf the commissars ruled.

In Nazi Germany a similar, but rightist, *Gleichschaltung* (coordination) of the institutions of the past would be implemented. All political and intellectual life would be brought under the close control of Hitler and the Nazi Party. The aristocracy would continue to exist, mainly to staff the higher officer ranks of the armed forces, but only if it gave absolute loyalty to Hitler and the Nazi dictatorship. The already strong German industrial economy would be harnessed for war, and its resources also applied to ethnic cleansing.

All that the revolutions, whether Communist or Nazi, accomplished was to create new elites. But born out of revolutionary conflict and impelled by radical ideology, these new elites created terror systems to keep themselves in power until as a result of defeat in war (1945), in the case of the Nazis, or economic collapse (1989), in the case of the Soviets, they were eliminated or forced to moderate their behavior.

The Nazi elite was succeeded in Germany by a group of industrialists and moderate politicians, most of whom got their start in the Nazi era. The former Soviet ruling class, which got its start under Stalinist Communism, today operates as a typical elite but without the terror system of the Stalinist era.

Elites endure longer when they tolerate criticism and mild political opposition and do not close themselves off entirely from new cultural trends. They retain for themselves a preponderance of wealth, a sufficient hold on political and legal systems, patronage of the arts, and a lavish lifestyle to which the middle class at times also aspires. This was true of Gaunt and his aristocratic group as it is true of the billionaire American capitalists of today.

The history of the twentieth century has taught us that a relatively open society, even if it allows great wealth and privilege to aristocrats or billionaire capitalists, operates more effectively and endures much longer than highly controlled and systematized societies. The latter either fall in overextended wars or collapse internally from economic malaise.

Successful societies need air to breathe and openness to function. Closed, totalitarian societies are potentially failing societies. The sloppiness and selfishness of a traditional elite is a social virtue because thereby totalitarianism is inhibited.

Gaunt was criticized in his day by the London street, the Parliamentary opposition, and the usual growling monastic chroniclers as being too forceful, domineering, lecherous, and selfish. He is criticized by some modern writers as being deficient in pursuit of clear policy goals, of being indecisive and a bit dilettantish, as well as of being selfish. But these qualities are characteristic of relatively open, durable elites in all times and places.

Gaunt left behind him specific important legacies: a royal

dynasty that ruled from 1399 to 1471, whose blood (albeit in diluted form) still runs in the veins of the British royal family; an enhanced regard for highborn women and for romantic love as it pertained to the aristocracy; the poetry of Chaucer made possible by Gaunt's early patronage; the emergence of English Protestantism following from his early protection of Wyclif.

Gaunt was not the great military leader and general his elder brother was reputed to be. He failed also in his scheme to make himself king of Castile. His grandson Henry the Navigator transformed Gaunt's aristocratic consciousness into the racist foundation of modern imperialism.

Above all, Gaunt's taste for war, his frenetic energy, and his physical strength, as well as his love of women and his wealth and lifestyle, set the model for European aristocratic behavior, which went unchallenged until the nineteenth century and is still the pattern for all effective and durable social elites.

⚬ᴍᴍᴍ⚬

"A high and strong culture is declining, but at the same time and in the same sphere new things are being born. The tide is turning, the tone of life is about to change."

These eloquent and historically significant sentences were published in 1924 in the English translation of Johan Huizinga's *The Waning of the Middle Ages,* first published in Dutch in 1919. Huizinga supervised the English translation of 1924, and the book was slightly abridged at that time. Nevertheless, in 1996 a translation of the unabridged version under the original title, *The Autumn of the Middle Ages,* was made.

Huizinga was a Dutch historical sociologist who taught at the University of Leyden. He published five books, including a sociology of play and a fascinating autobiography, in which he tells us that as a graduate student he played a leading role in organizing the first exhibition of the paintings of Vincent Van Gogh in his native Holland. Huizinga belonged to the flowering of late–nineteenth century European romanticism that is reflected in Van Gogh's postimpressionism.

In *The Waning of the Middle Ages* Huizinga examines "life, thought , and art" (mainly art) in Northern France and the Netherlands in the fourteenth and fifteenth centuries. Art in these countries in the thirteenth and fourteenth centuries explores Gothic "idealism," "symbolism," and "formalism." However, by the fifteenth century art becomes naturalistic in style, as medieval culture is now incapable of sustaining its "ethereal" qualities. It "solidifies and becomes rigid." Gothic culture has lost its capacity to convince and inspire. "Chivalry and hierarchy" have lost their dominance, as reflected in the transition from symbolism to naturalism. The once-glorious medieval culture, as shown in its art, is sliding into autumnal lack of confidence and decadence.

Huizinga's intellectual world cannot be reconstituted in our time. We have learned too much and experienced too much to go back to the 1920s. Yet there was always a vulnerability to Huizinga's thesis. He assumed that art history can be replicated and extended to a general paradigm of cultural and social change. However, there is another approach to art history—one that stresses narrow, technical reasons for stylistic modification and not the ramifications of broad-based cultural change. Nor is it clear why the shift from symbolism to naturalism should be expressive of rigidification. Naturalism could mean a transgressive liberation in evolving art styles.

The lifetime of John of Gaunt provides other indices of social and cultural transformation beyond art history. These are: Chaucer's quasi-secular humanism, Wyciff's proto-Protestantism, the entrenchment of a professional middle class of lawyers and bureaucrats, a market economy in land and the crushing of the peasantry under the wheels of capitalism, the negation of the legitimacy of sacred kingship, the instruments of parliamentary politics, the preponderance of infantry over armored cavalry.

"The tide is turning, the tone of life is about to change."

SOURCES

There are three modern works on John of Gaunt that are indispensable for his biography and provide a myriad of circumstantial details on his life. These are Sydney Armitage-Smith, *John of Gaunt* (London: Constable Press, 1904); P. E. Russell, *The English Intervention in Spain and Portugal in the Time of Edward III and Richard II* (Oxford: Clarendon Press, 1955); and, above all, Anthony Goodman, *John of Gaunt: The Exercise of Princely Power in Fourteenth-Century Europe* (New York: St. Martin's Press, 1992).

Armitage-Smith wrote his biography as a young man. He eschewed the academic life and became a government official. His biography of Gaunt is still valuable for its narrative flow. Russell ended up in the chair of Spanish and Portuguese at the University of London. His later articles, partly summarizing his massive *English Intervention* and supplementing it, are in his *Portugal, Spain, and the African Atlantic, 1343–1490: Chivalry and Crusade from John of Gaunt to Henry the Navigator and Beyond* (Brookfield, Vermont: Variorum, 1995).

Goodman, who is a professor of medieval history at the University of Edinburgh, set out to write the definitive biography of John of Gaunt. The result is somewhat less than that, being a series of studies mainly on Gaunt's political and military career but immensely valuable—British positivist scholarship at its best.

The second half of the fourteenth century, Gaunt's lifetime, was an era marked by revival of the great school of monastic historiography that had flourished at St. Albans Abbey in the early twelfth century (William of Malmesbury) and the mid-thirteenth century (Matthew Paris). Of the four clerical historians of the late fourteenth century, Henry Knighton, Thomas Walsingham, John de Trokelowe, and the anonymous monk of St. Albans, all but Knighton, who was a cathedral canon, were associated with St. Albans. Thomas Walsingham was the historiographical leader and may have written a large part of the chronicle attributed to Trokelowe. Walsingham was very interested in classical literature and his literary studies affected the dramatic kind of exposition in his historical writings.

It is a current consensus that of contemporary chroniclers in Gaunt's time, Thomas Walsingham is the best informed and most reliable. He compiled *Historia Anglicana,* 2 vols., ed. H. T. Riley (London: Rolls Series 1867–1868). But Walsingham is sharply inconsistent in his view of Gaunt—hostile at the start, more favorable as he goes along. This may simply be due to increased patronage the abbey received from Gaunt, but it may also be due to a reduction in Gaunt's support for Wyclif.

Of a different order is V. H. Galbraith, ed., *The Anonimalle Chronicle, 1333 to 1381* (Manchester: Manchester University Press, 1926), which provides eyewitness accounts of the Peasants' Revolt of 1381 and also of parliamentary debates in 1376. It was written by a London bureaucrat or possibly a merchant.

Along with the work of the chroniclers there are four volumes of Gaunt's business, political, and military letters: *John of Gaunt's Register, 1372–1376,* ed. Sydney Armitage-Smith, Camden 3rd series, vols. 20–21 (London: Royal Historical Society, 1911); *John of Gaunt's Register, 1379–1383,* ed. Eleanor C. Lodge and R.

Somerville, Camden 3rd series, vols. 56–57 (London: Royal Historical Society, 1937).

The most prolific historian writing in the Anglo-French world of the fourteenth century, Jean Froissart, *Oeuvres*, ed. K. de Lettenhove, 25 vols. (Brussels: V. Devaux, 1867–1877) has experienced fluctuations in his reputation over the past 125 years. Currently his reputation for accuracy is not very high. Froissart describes battles and events he did not witness. How assiduously he sought accurate knowledge from well-informed people is mysterious. His literary skill was high and he was very familiar with the royal and princely courts. In time, Froissart's work will be seen as a complex effort of the chivalric imagination. Of modest value is Adam de Usk, *Chronicon*, ed. E. M. Thompson (Oxford: Oxford University Press, 1904).

In spite of the skepticism expressed by some scholars with regard to the closeness of the relationship between John of Gaunt and the poet, government official, and diplomat Geoffrey Chaucer, three facts cannot be contraverted. First, Gaunt supported Chaucer with a sizable pension for three decades and even provided a smaller pension for Chaucer's wife, Philippa. Second, the paths of the Duke and the poet often crossed at the royal court for two decades. Third, Chaucer's sister-in-law Catherine Swynford was Gaunt's prime mistress, the mother of four of his children, and finally his third wife. One modern Chaucer biographer has suggested that Philippa Chaucer was also a ducal mistress.

Because of Gaunt's patronage of Chaucer, biographies of Chaucer illuminate Gaunt's life as well as Chaucer's thought world as it impinged from a more middle-class point of view on Gaunt's. The important works on Chaucer are Donald R. Howard, *Chaucer, His Life, His Works, His World* (New York: Dutton, 1987), a successful and imaginative effort at a full-scale biography written for the general reader; Derek Pearsall, *The Life of Geoffrey Chaucer: A Critical Biography* (Cambridge, Massachusetts: Blackwell, 1992), suffused with deep Harvard learning; Paul Strohm, *Social Chaucer* (Cambridge, Massachusetts: Harvard University Press, 1989), full of brilliant insights; John H. Fisher, *The Importance of Chaucer* (Carbondale: Southern Illinois University Press, 1992), of which much the same may be said. George Williams, *A New View of Chaucer* (Durham, North Carolina, Duke University Press, 1965), although it has not found favor with the academic establishment, is also worth reading.

The three works of Chaucer that are most relevant to John of Gaunt and his world are *The Canterbury Tales,* translated into modern English by Nevill Coghill (New York: Penguin, 1951, rev. ed., 1977); *Book of the Duchess;* and *Troilus and Criseyde.* Translations of the latter two works may be found in *The Complete Poetical Works of Geoffrey Chaucer,* translated by J.S.P. Tatlock and Percy MacKay (New York: Macmillan, 1928).

It is to the aristocratic world of chivalry that Gaunt belongs. He was perhaps its finest exemplar. Johan Huizinga's 1924 classic remains critically important: *The Waning of the Middle Ages* (reprint, New York: St. Martin's Press, 1969); or *The Autumn of the Middle Ages,* translated by Rodney J. Payton and Ulrich Mammitych (Chicago: University of Chicago Press, 1996). But more recent books offer fine insights on Gaunt's chivalric culture: Maurice H. Keen, *Chivalry* (New Haven: Yale University Press, 1984); and Richard W. Kaeuper, *Chivalry and Violence in Medieval Europe* (New York: Oxford University Press, 1999). Kaeuper's book is an attempt at a general sociology of chivalry.

F.R.H. Du Boulay, *An Age of Ambition* (New York: Viking Press, 1970), offers many fine insights into English society around

1400. The most dramatic event of Gaunt's lifetime, the Black Death of 1346–1349, is examined in all aspects in Norman F. Cantor, *In the Wake of the Plague: The Black Death and the World It Made* (New York: Free Press, 2001).

These are indispensable introductions to the political and social context in which Gaunt's life occurred: Maurice H. Keen, *English Society in the Later Middle Ages, 1348–1500* (London: Penguin, 1990); Stephen H. Rigby, *English Society in the Later Middle Ages: Class, Status, and Gender* (New York: St. Martin's Press, 1995); Michael Prestwich, *The Three Edwards* (London: Weidenfeld & Nicholson, 1980); W. M. Ormrod, *The Reign of Edward III* (New Haven: Yale University Press, 1990); John Hatcher, *Plague, Population and the English Economy, 1348–1530* (London: Macmillan, 1977); Christopher Dyer, *Standards of Living in the Later Middle Ages* (New York: Cambridge University Press, 1989); Clifford J. Rogers, ed., *The Wars of Edward III: Sources and Interpretations* (Rochester, New York: Boydell Press, 1999); Rodney H. Hilton, *Bond Men Made Free: Medieval Peasant Movements and the English Rising of 1381* (New York: Viking Press, 1973); Barbara W. Tuchman, *A Distant Mirror: The Calamitous Fourteenth Century* (New York: Alfred A. Knopf, 1978); Jonathan Sumption, *The Hundred Years War,* 2 vols. (Philadelphia: University of Pennsylvania Press, 1991–1999); Nigel Saul, *Richard II* (New Haven: Yale University Press, 1997); Michael Bennett, *Richard II and the Revolution of 1399* (Gloucestershire: Sutton, 1999), which connects Richard's sexuality and politics in a persuasive manner; Anthony Goodman and James Gillespie, eds., *Richard II: The Art of Kingship* (Oxford: Clarendon Press, 1999); Paul Strohm, *England's Empty Throne* (New Haven: Yale University Press, 1998); Alexander Rose, *Kings in the North: The House of Percy in British History*

(London: Weidenfeld & Nicolson, 2002); and John Gillingham, "From *Civilitas* to Civility: Codes of Manners in Medieval and Early Modern England," *Transactions of the Royal Historical Society,* 6th series, vol. 12, 2002, pp. 267–290.

On social history there are two important pioneering works: Zvi Razi, *Life, Marriage, and Death in a Medieval Parish: Economy, Society, and Demography in Halesowen, 1270–1400* (New York: Cambridge University Press, 1980); and Barbara H. Harvey, *Living and Dying in the Middle Ages* (New York: Oxford University Press, 1993). R. B. Dobson, ed., *The Peasants' Revolt of 1381* (New York: St. Martin's Press, 1970) is a well-edited collection of translated material.

Two important works on economic history are Christopher Dyer, *Making a Living in the Middle Ages: The People of Britain, 850–1520* (New Haven: Yale University Press, 2002); and Bruce M. S. Campbell, *English Seigneurial Agriculture* (New York: Cambridge University Press, 2000).

Gaunt's activity as a feudal lord is treated in Simon Walker, *The Lancastrian Affinity, 1361–1399* (Oxford: Clarendon Press, 1990). G. L. Harris, *Cardinal Beaufort: A Study of the Lancastrian Ascendancy and Decline* (Oxford: Clarendon Press, 1988) illuminates Gaunt's family connections and what happened to them in the next generation.

On literary, intellectual, and religious history, two works originally published in 1933 remain important: G. R. Owst, *Literature and Pulpit in Medieval England* (reprint, New York: Barnes & Noble, 1966); and Karl Young, *The Drama of the Medieval Church* (reprint, Oxford: Clarendon Press, 1967). In addition are three recent substantial works: Gordon Leff, *Bradwardine and the Pelagians* (Cambridge: Cambridge University Press, 1957; 1984);

Edward Grant, *The Foundation of Modern Science in the Middle Ages* (Cambridge: Cambridge University Press, 1996); Norman Kretzmann et al. eds., *The Cambridge History of Later Medieval Philosophy: From the Rediscovery of Aristotle to the Disintegration of Scholasticism, 1100–1600* (Cambridge: Cambridge University Press, 1982). Paul Binski, *Medieval Death: Ritual and Representation* (Ithaca, New York: Cornell University Press, 1996) is careful, learned, and insightful; Jean Delumeau, *Sin and Fear: The Emergence of a Western Guilt Culture, 13th to 18th Centuries* (New York: St. Martin's Press, 1991) is weird and verbose but interesting; Anne Hudson, ed., *Selections from English Wycliffite Writings* (Toronto: University of Toronto Press, 1997) has an extremely valuable introduction and notes; Caroline Walker Bynum and Paul Freedman, eds., *Last Things: Death and the Apocalypse in the Middle Ages* (Philadelphia: University of Pennsylvania Press, 2000) is also useful, particularly the paper by Laura A. Smoller.

On late medieval English religion in general, see Susan Brigden, *New Worlds, Lost Worlds: The Rule of the Tudors, 1485–1603* (New York: Viking, 2000), chapters 2 and 3; Miri Rubin, *Corpus Christi: The Eucharist in Late Medieval Culture* (Cambridge: Cambridge University Press, 1991); and Eamon Duffy, *The Stripping of the Altars: Traditional Religion in England, c. 1400–c. 1500* (New Haven: Yale University Press, 1992).

The best book on Piers Plowman is *William Langland's Piers Plowman: The C Version: A Verse Translation,* translated by George Economou (Philadelphia: University of Pennsylvania Press, 1996). James Simpson, *1350–1547: Reform and Cultural Revolution* (New York: Oxford University Press, 2002) contains many suggestive insights.

For Muslim and Jewish culture and society in Spain, Solomon

D. Goitein, *A Mediterranean Society: The Jewish Communities of the Arab World as Portrayed in the Documents of the Cairo Geniza,* 6 vols. (Berkeley: University of California Press, 1983–1993) supersedes all previous books on the subject. Goitein's *Mediterranean Society* was based on thirty years of archival research, and the significance of this mass of information has not yet been fully understood by medieval historians.

On Wyclif and the Lollards, who play a role tangential to Gaunt, Anne Hudson, *The Premature Reformation: Wycliffite Texts and Lollard History* (New York: Oxford University Press, 1988) is the starting point for all future research on the subject. It is based on a thorough study of all available sources. Herbert B. Workman, *John Wyclif: A Study of the English Medieval Church,* 2 vols. (Oxford: Clarendon Press, 1926), while out-of-date in several respects, still contains important material. K. B. McFarlane, *John Wycliffe and the Beginnings of English Nonconformity* (London: English University Press, 1952) is a classic that places Wyclif in the context of Oxford academic politics. On Gaunt as patron and protector of Wyclif, Joseph H. Dahmus, *The Prosecution of John Wyclif* (New Haven: Yale University Press, 1952) is valuable. Michael Wilks, *Wyclif: Political Ideas and Practice,* ed. Anne Hudson (Oxford: Oxbow Books, 2000), is a work of major importance based on decades of research.

For the biographer of Gaunt, Gaunt's relationships with Wyclif and Chaucer are important matters. Gaunt can be portrayed as the exemplar of aristocratic chivalry. But his appreciation for Chaucer's writings, as indicated by his steadfast patronage of the poet, and his stalwart protection of Wyclif show other sides to this very complex and transitional figure.

Index

BOOKS BY NORMAN F. CANTOR

THE LAST KNIGHT
ISBN 0-06-075403-6 (paperback)
Shakespeare put into Gaunt's mouth the most patriotic speech in the English language:
"...this sceptred isle. This other Eden, demi-paradise." In Cantor's capable hands, this
great man and those fascinating times are ready for their own starring roles.

ALEXANDER THE GREAT: *Journey to the End of the Earth*
ISBN 0-06-057012-1 (hardcover)
In this concise portrait of the great empire builder of the ancient world, Norman F.
Cantor explores Alexander's fascinating personal life as well as his military conquests.

ANTIQUITY: *From the Birth of Sumerian Civilization to the Fall of the Roman Empire*
ISBN 0-06-093098-5 (paperback)
Explores the social and cultural history, as well as the political and economic aspects,
from the birth of the Sumerian civilization to the fall of the Roman Empire.

CIVILIZATION OF THE MIDDLE AGES
ISBN 0-06-092553-1 (paperback)
A comprehensive general history on the Middle Ages that focuses on medieval culture
and religion.

IN THE WAKE OF THE PLAGUE: *The Black Death and the World It Made*
ISBN 0-06-001434-2 (paperback)
Cantor refutes common fallacies of the bubonic plague and presents recent
scientific discoveries and historical research to show the impact on society, religion,
and the Renaissance.

INVENTING THE MIDDLE AGES
ISBN 0-68-812302-3 (paperback)
Focuses on twenty great scholars of this century and how events in their lives and
spiritual and emotional outlooks shaped their interpretations of the Middle Ages.

MEDIEVAL READER
ISBN 0-06-272055-4 (paperback)
An anthology of letters, church and state documents, essays, poetry, ballads, and other
firsthand accounts of life and culture during the Middle Ages.

MEDIEVAL LIVES
ISBN 0-06-092579-5 (paperback)
Eight lively and engaging portraits of the men and women whose idealism exerted great
influence during the medieval era.

THE SACRED CHAIN: *The History of the Jews*
ISBN 0-06-092652-X (paperback)
A controversial, comprehensive account of the history of the Jewish people, rich in
sociological insight and historical as well as archaeological research.